Council for
Exceptional
Children

ELIZABETH
FARRELL

AND THE

HISTORY OF

SPECIAL EDUCATION

by
Kimberly Kode, Ph.D.
edited by Kristin E. Howard

Elizabeth Farrell and the History of Special Education

ISBN 0-86586-968-5

Copyright 2002 by Council for Exceptional Children, 1110 North Glebe Road, Suite 300, Arlington, Virginia, 22201-5704

Stock No. P5528 (individual)
Stock No. P5529 (bundle of 10)

Cover and layout, Kristin Howard

Printed in the United States of America

ᘓ

Now, my last work. The jails are full of your failures—all of you. Your state didn't ask you to be a teacher. You came and offered yourself as a teacher. And I want to challenge the right of any person to be a teacher of another unless that person will exhaust every resource to be a better and better teacher. If these men in jail - and the women, too - had had the kind of teachers that this government expected them to have, I question whether the jails would be full. I am aware that there is subnormality, psychotic conditions, poverty, and what not. But one of the greatest reasons is the lack of right educational opportunity.

I want every teacher here to think now of her failures, of the men and the women whose lives were cut short in their opportunity, because we were not well-trained enough, because the science of education was not an instrument in our hands. How many people are less than they should be because we lack the artistry of creating interest, because we lack the artistry of making attractive the knowledge of the world?

As we consecrate again, this moment, our lives to the education of this country, let us say with Wells "It is a race between destruction and education. I am a teacher, and destruction shall never win."

- Elizabeth E. Farrell

Foreword

At the headquarters of the Council for Exceptional Children, I often walk by a bronze plaque that bears the following inscription:

> In memory of Elizabeth Farrell, pioneer teacher of backward children in New York City. She devoted her life to the development of the ungraded classes and left to all children in need of special help the assurance that they might find it in the public schools.

But who was Elizabeth Farrell? I'm not sure many of us in the special education arena really know.

Elizabeth Farrell was a visionary, plain and simple. She invented the very concept of special education as we know it today. Over a century ago, she was challenged by assessment issues, teacher shortages, and inclusion. What can I say? The more things change, the more they stay the same.

Part of her vision was to continually address the challenges faced by those in the special education field while promoting fellowship and professionalism at the same time. In 1922 she was instrumental in establishing an organization that would do just that. That organization is our organization, the Council for Exceptional Children, and we thought it was time we put pen to paper and let our members know what an extraordinary woman Elizabeth was.

This book has given me a new reverence for the plaque outside my office door. We at CEC hope you will find this account of Elizabeth's work insightful and inspiring… and that you'll walk away knowing a little more about why you became a special educator.

Nancy D. Safer
Executive Director, Council for Exceptional Children

Prologue

Educating the Atypical Child: A Brief History

Although for centuries, people with disabilities were shunned, abandoned, and mistreated—in the late 18th and early 19th centuries progress began to be made. The first recorded attempt to teach a severely retarded child focused on a boy who had been seen running naked through the woods in France. Called the "Wild Boy of Aveyron," in 1798 he was caught, brought to Paris, and placed under the care of Dr. Jean Itard, the chief medical officer for the National Institute for the Deaf and Dumb. Dr. Itard, believing the boy's condition was curable, worked with him on reading and speaking. After 5 years, the boy, whom Dr. Itard named Victor, was only able to read and understand a few words, and Dr. Itard reluctantly ceased his work with him.

Other scientists of the time were also becoming interested in the treatment of people with disabilities. One of them, Dr. Edouard Seguin, was associated with Dr. Itard and later immigrated to the United States. Working with Dr. Samuel Howe, another special education pioneer, Dr. Seguin sought to initiate institutional care for people with disabilities. Together, both doctors organized institutional facilities in Massachusetts, Pennsylvania, Ohio, Connecticut, and New York.

However, in the early 1900s, attitudes in the United States regarding the treatment of these people took a considerable step backwards. In the midst of the era of Reconstruction following the Civil War, studies published by Richard Dugdale (1877) and Reverend Oscar McCulloch

(1888) associated people with disabilities with crime and poverty, and the role of institutions shifted from protecting those who are "different" from the public to protecting the public from those who are "different."

Indeed, one of America's most esteemed scientists, Dr. Henry Herbert Goddard, a contemporary of Elizabeth Farrell and a leader at the Vineland Training School for Feebleminded Boys and Girls in New Jersey, furthered this notion by concluding that retardation was genetically transmitted and perpetuated in families because of "bad blood." Scientists and governments alike called for "eugenics," a term coined by Sir Francis Galton in 1883 referring to a science that dealt with factors to improve the quality of the human race. Since retardation was thought to produce retardation, the fear was that evil, crime, and disease would spread if people with disabilities were allowed to procreate. In 1911 a group known as the Research Committee of the Eugenics Section of the American Breeder's Association recommended lifelong segregation and sterilization so that people with disabilities could not reproduce and pass on undesirable traits. Within 50 years, nearly 30,000 people with disabilities in the United States were sterilized.

Contents

Elizabeth E. Farrell

Introduction

History balances the frustration of "how far we have to go" with the satisfaction of "how far we have come." It teaches tolerance for the human shortcomings and imperfections, which are not uniquely of our generation, but of all time.

Lewis F. Powell, Jr.

Looking back over the history of education, and more specifically, the history of special education, it's easy for us to feel self-satisfied with the improvements in the treatment and education of people with disabilities made over the last 30 years. During this time, Public Law 94-142, the Education of All Handicapped Children Act, along with its reauthorization, the Individuals with Disabilities Education Act, were passed. Those laws, combined with the power of Public Law 101-336, the Americans with Disabilities Act, serve to focus the country and its citizens on the rights and needs of people with disabilities. Indeed, legislation and litigation over the past 30 years have done much to ensure that people with disabilities are treated with dignity and respect.

However, an examination of these improvements reveals that the groundwork for them was laid years before, often by educators whose names remain anonymous. In fact, this progress that we in the early 21st century are so eager to take credit for grew out of social and scientific factors that influenced education in America more than a century ago.

New York City's public school system was a forerunner in the education of people with disabilities, and at its helm was a first-generation

Welsh-Irish American schoolteacher. Even today, when so much of school reform originates at the administrative or university level and trickles down to the classroom, New York City is distinct in that its special education program began instead with one classroom in one school taught by one teacher, Elizabeth E. Farrell.

CHAPTER ONE:

Elizabeth's Background

Family and Foundations

Over two-and-a-half million immigrants arrived in America between 1840 and 1850, and Elizabeth Farrell's parents were among them. Unlike many immigrants of the time, however, Elizabeth's parents had a head start on their future. Skilled in the textile industry, the Farrell family was able to overcome many of the difficulties they faced as strangers in a foreign land and achieve financial security and economic success.

Michael Farrell, Elizabeth's father, arrived in America from Kilkenny, Ireland in 1848 when he was only 13 years old. The Farrell family settled in Catskill, New York, at the foot of the Catskill Mountains, a village made famous in 1800 by Washington Irving as the scene of Rip Van Winkle's legendary nap.

Elizabeth Farrell's mother, Mary Smith, also immigrated to the United States as a child. Born in Wales in 1838, she was the second oldest of six children, with her two youngest siblings born after the family arrived in the United States. The Smith family settled in Marcellus, New York, a small village in central New York State that served as home to several different woolen mills. Mary's father, David Smith, took a job as a spinner in the Marcellus Woolen Mill, and later Mary was trained as a weaver. It was probably the mill industry that brought Michael Farrell and Mary Smith together.

The Farrell family moved many times throughout central New York State as Michael Farrell took positions of increasing responsibility and pay at area mills, where he eventually became president of Central Mills Manufacturing in Utica. By 1877, Michael and Mary had six children, two boys and four girls. Elizabeth, born in 1870, was the oldest of the girls.

Elizabeth Becomes a Teacher

While growing up in Utica, Elizabeth was profoundly influenced by her own educators, the Sisters of Charity, who ran Utica Catholic Academy. This religious order was dedicated to nursing the sick, helping the needy, and educating children.

With increasing wealth and newfound affluence, Michael Farrell could afford to send Elizabeth to college. After her graduation from Utica Catholic Academy,

"America had a sizable group of educated women searching for self-satisfaction and a way to play a more important role in society than custom permitted..."

Elizabeth enrolled at the Oswego Normal and Training School (now the State University of New York at Oswego) to study teaching. Created in 1861 by Edward Austin Sheldon, the superintendent of city schools in

14

Oswego, its curriculum was based on Pestalozzi's "object" method. Sheldon had become dissatisfied with the results of the teacher training schools and sought a practical way to change the traditional book or lecture method to one where real objects are studied and the connections between school and life are explored. Sheldon's program became known as the "Oswego Movement," and Elizabeth graduated from the English degree program in 1895.

The Pestalozzian teaching philosophy at Oswego Normal and Training School would later prove to be the first of many important influences in her professional life. Years later Elizabeth discussed how she reflected on such ideas when creating the curriculum of the ungraded class:

> [T]o Pestalozzi we go to learn that our aim is not that the child should know what he does not know but that he should behave as he does not behave, and the road to right action is right feeling. And again he says: 'I have proved that it is not regular work that stops the development of so many poor children but the turmoil and irregularity of their lives, the privations they endure, the excesses they indulge in when opportunity offers; the wild rebellious passions so seldom restrained; and the hopelessness to which they are so often prey.'

After 2 years working in teacher training, Elizabeth accepted a position as a teacher in a small community near Utica known as Oneida Castle with a population of only 291 at the time of the 1900 census.

Elizabeth taught in a one-room schoolhouse, leaving after only a year to accept a teaching position in New York City.

Making a Difference

What compelled Elizabeth to leave the protective enclave her family created in central New York State and move to the slums of New York City? The conditions in the Lower East Side of Manhattan where she accepted her teaching position were certainly a radical departure from the environment in which she grew up. To speculate on Elizabeth's reasons it is necessary to examine the motivations of others involved in what was known as the Progressive Reform Movement. One theory, known as the Hofstadter or status thesis, suggests that Elizabeth's generation was the first sizable generation of American college graduates to come to maturity without clearly defined roles. In the publication, *From Poor Law to Welfare State: A History of Social Welfare in America*, author Walter Trattner describes the situation thusly:

> This was especially true for many young women who, if they wished to embark on a career, had few other useful activities open to them...As a result, America had a sizable group of educated women searching for self-satisfaction and a way to play a more important role in society than custom permitted...The complexity and challenge of the large city, however, offered them opportunities to create meaningful careers for themselves and at the same time

rescue society from the social ills resulting from rapid industrialization and urban change.

A similar explanation is offered by Arthur S. Link and Richard L. McCormick in their book, *Progressivism*. Link and McCormick submit that:

> Early 20th century social reform flowed from three well-springs of thought and motivation. One was the urge felt by certain middle- and upper-class men and women to help make urban life more just, tolerable, and decent. The second motivation was the drive of trained professionals to apply their knowledge and skills to social problems. The third motivation was the desire of many native-born Americans to use social institutions and the law to restrain and direct the unruly masses, many of whom were foreign-born or black.

Regardless of the motive behind Elizabeth's decision, after leaving Oneida Castle she found herself in a city in the midst of dramatic change.

ELIZABETH FARRELL AND THE HISTORY OF SPECIAL EDUCATION

CHAPTER TWO:

New York City, the Henry Street Settlement, and the First Special Education Class

❧

The Face of Change

When Elizabeth arrived in New York City in 1899, the United States was undergoing a period of profound change. With previous calls for manifest destiny fulfilled, America began to move toward its urban and industrial future, and in the period following the Civil War, cities grew rapidly. Developments in banking, railroads, and manufacturing allowed new industrialists like Morgan, Vanderbilt, Rockefeller, Carnegie, and others to amass untold amounts of wealth while the working class fell deeper into poverty. By 1860, it was estimated that the wealthiest 10% in America owned 70% of its wealth.

As manufacturing increased, the division of labor between the rich and poor widened in many urban areas. Business leaders of the time were more concerned about profits than the needs of their workers, often immigrants.

> *...a great number found themselves setting up new lives in the shantytowns and slums that mushroomed in various parts of the city.*

Political chaos on the European continent, combined with the potato famine in Ireland, drove huge waves of desperate people to America. Initially, these immigrants were mostly from western and northern European countries, with significant numbers of English, Irish, Germans, and Norwegians. Later, people from Eastern European countries—Hungary, Poland, and Czechoslovakia—as well as from Italy and Greece joined these, making urban areas such as New York City great melting pots. In fact, by the time the first decade of the 20th century had passed, nearly one seventh of New York City's population was foreign-born.

While some of these immigrants simply passed through New York to settle elsewhere, many were forced to remain. Lacking in both language and disposable income, a great number found themselves setting up new lives in the shantytowns and slums that mushroomed in various parts of the city. These immigrants, who had sought hope and fortune in America, merely shifted their living quarters from the ghettos in their home country to similar areas of poverty in urban New York City.

New York City: 1898

On January 1, 1898 the city had been restructured to create a metropolitan area of approximately 306 square miles. It included the boroughs of Manhattan, the Bronx, Brooklyn, Richmond County, and Long Island, as well as the cities of Newtown, Flushing, Jamaica, and Hempstead in the county of Queens. As a result of this restructuring there was a net increase of approximately 5% of the city's student population, making the City of New York now responsible for the education of almost half a million pupils.

Tenement room in Manhattan's
Lower East Side

This new district saw a need for teachers in parts both comparatively sparse and densely populated, and there was no part of New York City more densely populated than Manhattan's Lower East Side. By 1893, 1.5 million human beings lived in this congested neighborhood and it became the most notorious slum area in the city. Millions of people made that corner of New York their first—and sometimes last—stop. Lillian Wald, who was to become a prominent figure in Elizabeth's life, described the living conditions:

> They were packed into dank, airless tenement rooms like ramshackle pieces of furniture in a warehouse. These firetraps they called homes had broken-down stairs, evilsmelling outdoor toilets, rarely a bathtub, and often no running water. The streets…were crammed with shops, pushcarts, and peddlers hawking …bargains…The hectic commerce was interlaced with piles of rotting garbage, horsedrawn wagons, and fire escapes strewn with household possessions.

For those in New York lucky enough to live elsewhere, the Lower East Side represented an alarming, dark side of the city that they chose not to acknowledge. It was a foreign city within their city, and were it not for opportunities to exploit it, politically and economically, most New Yorkers seemed indifferent to it.

Wald and her colleagues at the Henry Street Settlement dealt with the Lower East Side immigrant population daily.

Lillian Wald and the Henry Street Settlement

The same could not be said for Progressive Reformer Lillian Wald, however. Working with Mary Brewster, a like-minded classmate from New York Hospital's School of Nursing, Wald founded the Henry Street Settlement in the center of the Lower East Side. This was one of the first settlement houses in American history. Built on the belief that living and working in the community was the most effective way to improve social conditions, Wald and her colleagues at the Henry Street Settlement dealt with the Lower East Side immigrant population daily.

Working from a background in nursing, the main focus for Wald and Brewster was the prevention and treatment of health problems, but when increasing numbers of neighborhood children were being kept out of school due to ill health, their interest in education grew. Thus, it was inevitable that they take a vital interest in New York's public education system. Their involvement in Public School Number One, the Henry Street School, became an increasing focus.

ELIZABETH FARRELL AND THE HISTORY OF SPECIAL EDUCATION

The Henry Street School

Founded by the women of the Society of Friends in 1802, the Henry Street School faced a multitude of challenges. In 1899 the Compulsory Education Provision had passed, stating that all children between the ages of 8 and 12 must attend school from October to June and that children between the ages of 12 and 14 could work only if they attended school at least 80 days. This new provision meant that those children, who earlier had spent their time working or on the streets, would now be forced to attend school. Many schools were not equipped to handle such a large number of students, and by June of that year, there were over 2,200 pupils at the Henry Street School, making it so overcrowded that many students were only able to attend part-time.

Further, with a student enrollment largely made up of those children that lived within the immediate neighborhood, teachers faced a student population with a variety of needs, many of which were beyond the scope of what they had been trained to deal with. Often these children had several strikes against them before they ever entered the school doors: some spoke little or no English; some had physical or mental problems that interfered with their learning; and some had only attended school erratically. Unable to meet the instructional and behavioral needs of many of these students, teachers throughout New York City struggled to find a means of coping.

One of Wald's main concerns was the education of children at the Henry Street School, and in 1899 she began to hear of a teacher's work at that school. This teacher, as it was reported to Wald by a settlement resident, had "ideas." Intrigued, Wald sought an acquaintance with the teacher, Elizabeth E. Farrell. Those "ideas," combined with the support of Wald and the Henry Street Settlement, developed into the first coordinated attempt to educate atypical* children.

Rethinking the System

As a teacher at the Henry Street School, Elizabeth's work was cut out for her. She described her first class under Principal William L. Ettinger as one which "grew out of conditions in a neighborhood furnished in

Progressive Reformer Lillian Wald became a prominant figure in Elizabeth's life

many serious problems in truancy and discipline." Comprised only of boys between the ages of 8 and 16 years old, most had been unsuccessful in the regular education classes where, as the City Superintendent of Schools reported, they had encountered "ordinary means of teaching...where intellect is appealed to directly requiring of the child the ability to think in the abstract." Some were considered "incorrigible" and unwilling to follow school rules; others were frequently truant; some could neither read nor count; others were several years retarded* in their grades, and many had health problems that interfered with their school attendance and ability to learn. As Elizabeth noted in her article, "Special Classes in the New York City Schools,"(1906, 1907) "...school, as they found it, had little or nothing for them." They had "set themselves against what society had organized for their welfare, the educational system."

Indeed, the paradigm in use in the schools of New York City did little to address students' individual differences or learning problems. In J. M. Rice's, *The Public School System of the United States* (1893), the author observed the teaching of over 1,200 teachers in the schools of 36 cities and noted that schools "...aim to do little, if anything beyond crowding the memory of the child with a certain number of cut-and-dried facts..." Rice further observed that:

> The typical New York City primary school...is nevertheless a hard, unsympathetic, mechanical-drudgery school, a school in which the light of science has not yet entered. Its characteristic features lie in the severity of discipline, a discipline of enforced silence, immobility, and mental passivity.

Maintaining that education should be based on providing "...the child the right education—the kind of training which he needs, therefore which he accepts," Elizabeth had some ideas as to how the curriculum could be organized to keep her students interested in school while more fully addressing their needs. Prior to asking the School Board to fund any special instruction districtwide, however, she wanted to develop and monitor the success of one class based on her curricular suppositions. Thus, she began to experiment with the structure and dynamics of her own class.

During this critical period of development, Elizabeth sought guidance and support from several different sources: her principal, William L. Ettinger; Superintendent William H. Maxwell; Charles Burlingham, president of the Board of Education; and Felix Warburg, a member of both the Boards of Education and the Henry Street Settlement. It was under their watchful eyes that Elizabeth was given the freedom to examine various methods of teaching and make decisions regarding what worked best in her classroom with her pupils.

> *her curricular model was completely individualized, pragmatic, and free from preconceived lesson structure.*

Elizabeth Creates Her First Special Education Curriculum

Not the result of any theory on learning or retardation, her curricular model was completely individualized, pragmatic, and free from preconceived lesson structure. Indeed, she believed in the strength of a curriculum based on the varying needs of each one of her students. Elizabeth noted she looked forward to the time:

> when every teacher will know what the ability of the child is, and the child's burden as it is represented by the course of study he undertakes. That burden will be trimmed to his ability. It will not be the same burden for every child, but it will be a burden for every child commensurate with his ability to bear.

Elizabeth Farrell and the History of Special Education

Intended to exploit the potential of multi-age grouping that she had witnessed while teaching in rural Oneida Castle, Elizabeth wanted to treat learning in a holistic manner, building on each individual student's experiences. She felt that the students "...had to be shown that school could be more than mere study of books in which they had no interest. They had to be convinced that to attend school was a privilege not a punishment."

To change this perception, Elizabeth used a variety of nontraditional supplies to teach the boys in her class, stating that:

> ...instead of books, they had tin cans; instead of spellers, they had picture puzzles to solve; instead of penmanship lessons, they had watercolor paints and brushes; instead of arithmetic and multiplication tables, they had wood and tools, and things with which to build and make.

She believed the ungraded* classes needed to "...appeal to the constructive, the acquisitive, the imitative instincts in the child..." and be "...full of things to do, full of interesting activities to pursue, full of constructive activity."

Lydia Chace, in her 1904 report to the National Conference of Charities and Corrections, observed this while visiting Elizabeth's class:

> The class has been a difficult one to teach; in the first place, it has usually numbered eighteen or twenty; then the boys have been very ungraded, at times, some more wayward than backward. At present, there are nineteen in the class, twelve of whom are mentally deficient. The youngest is six and a half years of age and the oldest seventeen. In work they range

* see glossary

from "sub-kindergarten" to the second year of the grammar school. Notwithstanding these difficulties, each child is studied individually and his education is fitted to his needs.

The chief aim is to create in the boys a love of work so that when they go out into the world, they will not join the ranks of the criminal class. For this reason, everything is related to manual training and made subordinate to it. They always have some subject as a center; at present it is the farm. In woodwork, they are making a house and barn, fences, furniture, and flower-boxes. They are weaving the rugs for the floor, making a hammock, doing raffia work and basketry. They went to the country for the soil to plant their miniature fields, and sent to Washington for seeds. In painting, their subjects have been apple blossoms and violets with an illustrated trip to Bronx Park. In picture study, they have taken "Oxen Plowing," "The Angelus," etc. In arithmetic, the older boys measure in a concrete way, the rooms of the house and the fields. In their written work in English, they are having stories of farm life, and reports of personal observation; in reading, stories of dogs, horses, making hay, and so on; in spelling, words relating to manual occupations, e.g., "soil, seeds, leaves, barn." In nature work, they are studying soils, the earthworm, buds and seeds. This is simply suggestive of the excellent work that the boys are taking up at present. The subjects are chosen and the different studies related to the center with the purpose of developing the social instincts in the boys.

Elizabeth Farrell and her first ungraded class

Years later when speaking to a summer school class at the University of Pennsylvania, Elizabeth explained her rationale in designing such an unusual curriculum:

> The school now more than ever must compete with its only real competitor, the street. To fail would be to acknowledge that the fortuitous education of the street must always and ever count for more in a child's life than the well-ordered, logical, and psychologically adapted regime of formal education. The problem thus becomes analytic. What is the attraction of the streets? First and foremost is the constantly changing activity. The boy is never bored by street life. When one thing ceases to attract, it is pushed aside and he attends to the new and interesting. The activity goes from

hanging onto wagons with its consequent danger and interest, to listening to street musicians with their bright, catchy
tunes.

Elizabeth Moves Into the Henry Street Settlement House

Elizabeth's curricular model worked. Word of her classroom suc-
cesses quickly spread and it wasn't long before she moved into the
Settlement House, becoming a trusted friend and ally to Lillian Wald for
the next 25 years.

At the House, Wald surrounded herself with middle-class women with
no ties to husbands or children, women who could fully devote their ener-
gies to their work within the Henry Street community, and Elizabeth fit
right in. Years later Wald described the importance the Settlement House
and community had on Elizabeth's visions for education: "...Farrell insist-
ed she found in the House a living spring of inspiration..." that "...the
Settlement's rich understanding of people, life, events, its multicolored and
changing activities, provided her with a background which helped keep her
own thought and emotion fresh and vital."

Wald encouraged Elizabeth's work with children and assisted her in
refining her theory of special instruction. She helped provide equipment
not yet on the School Board's requisition list and is credited with per-
suading the New York City School Board in 1902 to hire the first school
nurse.

Most importantly, however, Lillian Wald worked to interest School Board members and others in Elizabeth Farrell's work.

Henry Street Settlement Nurse on
assignment in the Lower East Side

CHAPTER THREE:

The Special Education Experiment

Beyond Henry Street: Piquing the Interest of the New York City School Board

With Wald as her mentor, members of the Board of Superintendents began to take a particular interest in Elizabeth's program. Before recommending any general rule to establish special instruction for similar atypical children throughout the district, however, the Board thought it best to experiment in several schools with classes affording various courses of study or other special features. Superintendent William Maxwell agreed, recommending that "no very extensive schema be adopted" since "mistakes will certainly be made in any attempt to solve the extremely delicate problem before us, and that mistakes are much more easily corrected when the field of experiment is small than when it is large."

Thus, several classes modeled after Elizabeth's design were established in Manhattan at Public Schools Numbers 40, 77, 113, 111, and 180, and all were studied closely. By 1903 there were 10 such classes in both Manhattan and the Bronx, and the number of classes seemed likely to increase further.

Motives From the School Board

Why, we might easily ask, did Elizabeth receive such interest and support for a segment of the population that was largely ignored in a have-and-have-not society? Not surprisingly, the rationale used by the Board for establishing such a program districtwide was largely monetary. Elizabeth noted that:

> ten percent of the school budgets of this country are spent in re-teaching children that which they have once been taught but have failed to learn. The educational budget for this country is four hundred millions of dollars. Forty millions of it is spent each year in re-teaching retarded children.

Further, numerous children were dropping out of school without learning a trade, and it was believed that the majority of criminals and victims of crime were recruited from this group. With the goal of preventing a large population of unskilled labor being forced into a criminal class, it was necessary to sustain children's interest in school. Maxwell summed up the objective clearly when stating "the best of all ways to abolish truancy is to make schools so attractive that children will not willingly be absent."

...the rationale used by the Board for establishing such a program districtwide was largely monetary.

Therefore, the impetus for classes such as Elizabeth's wasn't entirely altruistic. With exceptional children present in the already large classes, many felt that not only did the atypical child degenerate, but that the class was hindered as well, and the teacher's work was made harder and less effective. A 1918 *New York Times* article summarized the thoughts of the time by stating:

> Besides getting nothing in the way of educational training themselves, these children have served as a drawback to the work of the rest of the class. It is an unfortunate phase of almost every school system that the class goes ahead only as fast as the slowest.

Even Elizabeth's mentor, Lillian Wald, in her book, *The House on Henry Street*, confirmed as much, noting that "the settlement gladly helped her develop her theory of separate classes and special instruction for the defectives*, not alone for their sakes, but to relieve the normal classes which their presence retarded."

Perfecting Her Special Education Program

By 1903, there were at least 10 special classes modeled after Elizabeth's, and the number seemed likely to increase exponentially. As the unofficial expert regarding these classes, Elizabeth continued to seek additional information so as to allow her to further refine her practices. To that end, she requested a leave of absence for the month of June 1903 so that she could study the teaching methods other countries used for their atypical children.

* see glossary

Supporting her in her efforts to better educate herself regarding the special class, Superintendent Maxwell urged the Board of Education to grant her request and provide her with letters of introduction. To comply with the Board of Education by-laws, however, either the Board of Education or the Board of Superintendents had to make a formal request of Elizabeth. The Chairman of the Committee on Elementary Schools, J. W. Mack, therefore, made a formal request that she visit schools abroad for the "purpose of examining into the instruction of deficients and atypicals..." and submit a report to the Committee on Elementary Schools upon her return.

Studying Special Classes Abroad

In 1891 the School Board of London, England, had adopted a resolution stating "special schools for those children who, by reason of physical or mental defect, cannot be properly taught in the ordinary standards or by ordinary methods, be established..." and an inspector was appointed by the national government to oversee this work. Eight years later in 1899, the National Board of Education investigated the special school program, the result of which was an amendment to the Elementary School Law of 1870 which provided national recognition and help for certified schools for such children. By 1903, the year Elizabeth traveled there, Great Britain had 10 years of experience working with these special classes and schools.

In Great Britain, systematic inspection revealed that 1% of the children attending school were considered physically or mentally defective, and Elizabeth found the ways children were identified and assigned to these schools to be extremely methodical. Teachers, working under the supervision of a superintendent of special schools, first inspected all school children to determine if any appeared to suffer from physical or mental defects. The findings were then reported to the Superintendent of the Instruction of Physically and Mentally Defective Children who, along with a medical officer, examined the child. If the report was found to be correct, the child was sent to one of the centers for the instruction of defective children. In completely separate programs with separate facilities, doctors regularly examined these children, and extensive records were kept.

> *The idea of a completely separate educational program proved unsettling for Elizabeth, however, and the experience made her question "what particular kind of child could be educated only in a special class?"*

The idea of a completely separate educational program proved unsettling for Elizabeth, however, and the experience made her question "what particular kind of child could be educated only in a special class?" Upon her return to New York, Elizabeth submitted, as was requested, her "Report on the Treatment of Defective Children in Great Britain," published in the Board of Education's *Fifth Annual Report* in 1903. Aware that in the initial stages, the London public had been opposed to offering these kinds of educational programs, she wrote that "...It is the boast of Americans that every child has the opportunity of school education but it is true that many children—through no fault of their own—get nothing from education. Not education but the right education should be our boast."

Her experiences in Great Britain became the foundation for many of her future decisions regarding the ungraded classes. In fact, her decision to turn away from the concept of special schools and instead embrace the notion of classes within the public schools may have been cemented by what she observed in Great Britain. Further, observing the large number of mentally defective children suffering from "most positive and pronounced" physical problems may have planted the idea for the creation of the Psycho-Educational Clinic. Capitalizing on the insight gained from her study of Great Britain's system, Elizabeth continued her work in the ungraded class on Henry Street, further refining her ideas and putting them into practice in her own classroom. As a result, her name would become synonymous with this type of special instruction.

> *...her decision to turn away from the concept of special schools and instead embrace the notion of classes within the public school may have been cemented by what she observed in Great Britain.*

CHAPTER FOUR:

Elizabeth's Special Education Model Takes Hold

Extending Special Education in the
New York City Public Schools

In his 1905 *Seventh Annual Report to the Board of Education*, Superintendent William H. Maxwell declared: "The time of experiment is now ended—the ungraded classes have fully justified their existence—and for the future there remains...the wide extension of this system." Thus, the Board of Education, with Superintendent Maxwell as its driving force, officially sanctioned the ungraded class program on February 14, 1906, and appointed Elizabeth Inspector of the Ungraded Class Department. With that designation, New York City became the first American city where this type of program was one person's sole responsibility. Ordered to report directly to the Board of Superintendents, she had an extensive list of duties, including supervising the existing ungraded classes, aiding in the formation of new classes, cooperating in the examinations of children proposed for admittance to or removal from ungraded classes, assigning pupils, training teachers for these classes, and recommending teachers for 3-month leaves of absence to study the training of mental defectives.

To provide both Elizabeth and school principals a framework from which to operate, Maxwell issued several instructions regarding the special classes. While leaving the exact subject matter largely up to the school principals, Maxwell stated that "under no circumstances are drawing and physical training to be eliminated," further advising that

> *"...[the teacher] should be wise and tactful, not only with children but with adults, for if she is to succeed, she must become the friend and adviser of the family..."*

"girls 12 years of age or older should have instruction in sewing and cooking, and boys 12 years of age or older should be taught woodworking and the use of tools." Maxwell also encouraged principals to obtain qualified individuals to lead these unique classes, stating:

> The teacher who is to take up this work should be peculiarly adapted to it by nature. She should have insight into child nature, affection for children, and ability for leadership. She should be resourceful and inventive, reaching and quickening the spirit of those who suffer. She should be wise and tactful, not only with children but with adults, for if she is to succeed, she must become the friend and adviser of the family, in order to get the co-operation so necessary to the best work of the child. She must be sanguine, cheerful, optimistic, patient, and have infinite capacity for taking pains.

An Early Proponent of Inclusion

This framework aside, Elizabeth's new position forced her to make many immediate decisions about the structure and future role of the ungraded class, not the least of which was determining whether or not to follow Great Britain's lead in creating completely separate classes in separate schools. Noting that the special school's focus was on "preventing the association in school of the mentally defective and the so-called normal child," Elizabeth decided to continue establishing special classes within existing schools, concluding that:

> The special school with its 'separateness' emphasized in its construction, in its administration, differentiates, sets aside, classifies, and of necessity stigmatizes the pupils whom it receives. How could it be otherwise? Mental subnormality is so often associated with lack of beauty, proportion, and grace in the physical body of the child, the way we say mental subnormality and physical anomalies go hand-in-hand. Now bring together a rather large group—a hundred such children—and there assembled countless degrees of awkwardness and of slovenliness; infinite variations in overdevelopment or in arrested development and a dozen other mute witnesses of a mind infantile or warped. It would be next to impossible to save these helpless ones from the jibes of a not too kind world. The school which is to serve best must conserve the moral as well as the mental, the spiritual as well as the physical nature of the pupil.

Grade School Class, early 1900s

In fact, Elizabeth wanted the ungraded pupils to have the best of both worlds: "the opportunity for individual instruction while it presents to him, when he is able to grasp it, the chance of doing class work." She provided an illustration of how such an arrangement would work, foreshadowing the delivery of special education services to thousands of American schoolchildren years later:

> A child, hopelessly unable to comprehend even the simplest truths of arithmetic and further handicapped by a speech defect, which prohibited his taking part in a recitation period requiring spoken language, was found to have more than ordinary ability and interest in reading. The ungraded teacher was able to help him along the line of his interests. When he was able to write his answers he could attend a sixth-year class for those studies in which he could excel. His own self-respect and the increased prestige of the ungraded class were the result of his excellent work. In many schools the upper grade children are invited to visit the ungraded classroom to see the manual training exhibit. The children who were in danger of being pseudo-intellectual snobs because of scholastic achievements, realized when viewing the excellence of work identical with their own shopwork exercises, that to each has been given a talent, and that this group of "different" children have contributions to make to the life of the school no less valuable because they are unlike.

CHAPTER FIVE:

Assessment Challenges

Who Gets In? Problems With Assessment

With the ungraded class program now an official part of the educational system in the City of New York, Elizabeth faced an increasing number of children being referred for special class placement, and she struggled to determine exactly which children might benefit from this kind of individualized instruction. Referrals came from a variety of sources: teachers and principals, physicians, the Bureau of Attendance, the Department of Physical Training, the Red Cross, and Children's Court, as well as the city's Department of Health. Those recommended for inclusion suffered from a wide variety of behavioral, academic, physical, or psychological problems and included nervous children who cried easily, were easily frightened, constantly moved, had unusual anxieties, or were epileptics; psychopathic children who did not play or played with children much younger than themselves; overconscientious children who exhibited irritability or a marked change in disposition; children with gross conduct disorders, including the truant, the incorrigible, and those who had tantrums; "morally defective" children who exhibited criminal tendencies; and those children whose progress in school was considered unsatisfactory or retarded.

The 1899 Compulsory Education Provision meant that those children who earlier had spent their time working or on the streets, would now be forced to attend school. Many schools were not equipped to handle the new deluge of students

Further compounding the problem, in 1903 an additional component of the Compulsory Education Provision was passed, requiring all children to attend school until 14 years of age. The law stated that all children between the ages of 14 and 16 had to attend school unless employed, and all boys between the ages of 14 and 16 who leave school for employment prior to completing the elementary school course must attend 16 weeks of evening school. Those in violation could be sent to truant/probationary schools for up to 2 years or until age 16, and their parents could be fined for failure to keep them in school. Although this law was not consistently enforced, it served to further increase the number of students referred to Elizabeth's program.

Originally concerned with children who didn't seem to "fit," irrespective of the cause, Elizabeth and the Board of Education began to focus more and more on those children whose low mentality, measured on intelligence tests between 50 and 75, prevented them from benefiting from any type of regular class instruction. Relying on estimates that anywhere between 1% and 10% of the population were of low mentality, Elizabeth and others calculated that between 5,000 - 10,000 children in New York City would then be eligible for ungraded classes. By 1905 those estimates changed, and it was theorized that between 6,000 - 12,000 children in New York City schools were unable to handle the normal course work required of them in the regular classes.

> *In a manner that seems reflective of the kinds of self-contained special education classes offered today, Elizabeth refined the ungraded classes even further, designing different classes to more appropriately meet the needs of the students.*

In a manner that seems reflective of the kinds of self-contained special education classes offered today, Elizabeth refined the ungraded classes even further, designing different classes to more appropriately meet the needs of the students:

> Ungraded classes differ in type. They are organized on the basis of chronological age as well as of mental age. There are classes for older high grade girls, classes for younger children, and so on. It is possible to differentiate ungraded classes on the principle of the children's most insistent need—classes for neurotic children, classes for psychopathic children, trade extension classes for girls.

Initial Assessment Methods

The initial method for selecting which children qualified for placement in the ungraded class program was established by the Board of Education. Principals reported to Elizabeth any child who, in the opinion of the teacher, Department of Health, or Department of Physical Training, was unable to do regular class work due to mental deficiency or any child 3 or more years retarded in school. Retardation was determined according to the criterion established by the city superintendent: a student entering 1st grade at 6 or 7 years of age and progressing through the grades would be as follows:

First grade	6-8 years
Second grade	7-9 years
Third grade	8-10 years
Fourth grade	9-11 years
Fifth grade	10-12 years
Sixth grade	11-13 years
Seventh grade	12-14 years
Eighth grade	13-15 years

The teacher then completed a card with information based on her observations of the student as well as any possible circumstances that might influence the child's condition: the economic condition of the family; home life; kindergarten attendance; number of terms in grade; school history; school attendance; required work; general knowledge; powers of attention and memory; motor control; and habits of anger, obstinacy, cruelty, and truthfulness. The record was next filed with Elizabeth's office, and the school principal was advised on the child's examination date; their dates were made in each district only once every 6 months.

These examinations, conducted by Elizabeth and the physician assigned to her department, when combined with the teacher's report, often yielded information that was useful to the regular teacher, although the student might not be suited for the ungraded class. Elizabeth provided an example of such a case in her *1907 Annual Report to the Board of Education*:

> An undersized, nervous, elf-like girl of nine years, she could keep awake and alert, except when required to sit at her desk. The moment she was still, her head was down and school forgotten; sleep would overpower her. Here was, indeed, a strange condition—a child apparently well, sleeping early in the school day. A word or two brought out the fact that this child, a mere baby, was required to rise at five o'clock in the morning, to sew buttons on boy's trousers until school time; after school in the afternoon, she was again compelled to take up the burden and work far into the night. This child knew that two different sizes of buttons were used, knew where to place them; she knew that ten buttons were put on one pair of trousers and twenty on two, but beyond that she could not go. This child was not a case for the ungraded class. The child had ability but it was used up each day before school received her. The fact of sleeping, in this particular case, was due to fatigue. Nature was doing her work; school had to wait. The fact, however, that this peculiarity was noted saved the child. It

was found upon investigation that the father was saving his earnings, while his wife and this child were providing food and shelter for him and one younger child.

While Elizabeth acknowledged this referral process provided a "clear, comprehensive idea of the child, and his proper place," she ultimately viewed it as unsatisfactory as it left the selection of children to opinion and chance. By relying on this method, undue numbers of children with conduct disorders who were not mentally defective were referred to the program, while there was a complete absence of referrals for quiet, unobtrusive children, whom she felt were often overlooked due to "goodness." Further, some school principals failed to refer students at all. In 1908, the second year of Elizabeth's department's existence, only 116 of 180 Manhattan schools reported, only 12 of 42 in the Bronx reported, and only 74 of 148 Brooklyn schools reported any students for potential placement in the ungraded classes.

> *...undue numbers of children with conduct disorders who were not mentally defective were referred to the program, while there was a complete absence of referrals for quiet, unobtrusive children, whom she felt were often overlooked due to "goodness."*

To Elizabeth this represented a serious administrative problem. Wanting every school to know "the extent of its problem of mental abnormality," she longed for a more consistent manner of identifying and placing students in the ungraded classes, believing a satisfactory method must be based on the elimination of chance, opinion, and emotional factors. In her *Annual Report to the Board of Education* (1918-1920), Elizabeth noted with some dismay that "...it is obvious that we are not identifying all the mentally defective children in the schools...due to the inherent weaknesses in the present method of selecting children for examination..."

Standardizing Selection: Development of the Psycho-Educational Clinic

As Inspector of the Department of Ungraded Classes, Elizabeth worked to create a referral procedure that would both meet her criteria and correctly place only those children with low mentality in the special classes. Originally examining children referred for the ungraded classes once a week in Manhattan and Brooklyn at "clinic days," she fought yearly for additional monies to fund more supervisory and medical staff positions. After the Board of Education approved her request in 1913, she started refining responsibilities and procedures to make testing and placement decisions more objective, establishing the Psycho-Educational Clinic.

Part of the Department of Ungraded Classes, the clinic's function was to reveal any underlying factors in the maladjustment of school children. The Psycho-Educational Clinic employed personnel from four different fields: psychology, social services, medicine, and education, all of whom worked together to determine which children were best served with placement in the ungraded department and which children could be best served through other means.

Each professional within the clinic performed a specific function. In an effort to determine the student's rate of learning as well as their positive and negative personal attributes, the psychologists administered both the Seguin and Binet intelligence tests and the New York Regents Literacy Test. Results from both tests were then compared to reports from teachers. Individual exams, including the Pintner-Patterson Performance Test, the Haggerty Intelligence Exam Delta II, the Trabue Language Complete Scales B and C, the Woody-McCall Mixed Fundamentals in Arithmetic, and the Thorndike-McCall Reading, were administered only to those who scored below 70 or exhibited marked irregularity in the group intelligence exams, were below grade 3A, were of foreign-birth and in school long enough to have learned English but had failed to make satisfactory progress, and to those suffering from partial or complete deafness. Believing they had inaugurated a new method of selecting children for special education, Elizabeth maintained this was a more scientific way of selecting students to receive services.

The medical inspectors were responsible for examining all children proposed for placement in the ungraded classes. Working to determine the basis of any nervous or mental disease, they often recommended the first line of treatment. They looked as well for evidence of contagious diseases, including ringworm, impetigo, scarlet fever, scabies, diphtheria, measles, chicken pox, pertussis, mumps, or tuberculosis, and sought to identify any physical defects that might impede school progress. Testing by the medical inspectors revealed that 90% of the children examined for placement in the ungraded classes were found to suffer from some form of physical defect. Not all children with physical defects found their way into the ungraded classes, however. If it was determined that the child was prevented from learning due to the physical defect rather than low mentality, and it was possible to treat the

defect, then it was treated while the child remained in the grade so that he or she could return to normal work.

Medical inspectors also had the responsibility of periodically re-examining all ungraded children. Elizabeth felt it was absolutely essential that the ungraded class children be re-examined by a doctor regularly to ascertain the progress of the child and to furnish data for recommendations for discharge, exclusion, or promotion. She noted that removals from the ungraded classes were made for three reasons: on the recommendation of the school principal that the child is ready to do grade level work; when the child is 16 years old and is no longer required according

If it was determined that the child was prevented from learning due to the physical defect rather than low mentality, and it was possible to treat the defect, then it was treated while the child remained in the grade so that he or she could return to normal work.

51

to compulsory attendance laws to attend school; or if it is determined that the child is suitable for institutional care.

Visiting teachers employed in the Psycho-Educational Clinic fulfilled a social worker function. Initially volunteers performed a variety of services for the clinic: analyzing home conditions; securing information from interviews regarding the child's early life; obtaining parental cooperation; discussing problems with teachers and principals; assisting ungraded teachers; and summarizing and following up on clinic recommendations. Additionally, they worked closely with social service agencies to get families registered and help them get financial help and medical care. Elizabeth discussed the work of the visiting teacher in *Aiding the Backward Child* (1927):

> The visiting teacher learns about the child's life outside school. If he wants to hike, or join classes or neighborhood clubs, she arranges it. Then an effort is made to improve the child's physical condition, and sometimes, to educate the parents.

Despite the important function visiting teachers performed, there were very few employed in the clinic. In 1913-1914 the Psycho-Educational Clinic had only two visiting teachers serving approximately 3,000 children. By 1920-1921, the number of children needing assistance rose to approximately 6,000, yet there were still only three visiting teachers attached to the clinic. Despite Elizabeth's repeated requests, the Board of Education made few provisions for additional visiting teachers. As a result, the existing visiting teachers could handle only the most urgent of cases, and principals and teachers often hesitated to involve them until the problem became severe. Elizabeth estimated that to adequately serve the children and families in need, an additional 200 visiting teachers were required.

Based on the results of all of the Psycho-Educational Clinic examinations, decisions were then made about which manner of treatment and placement would be appropriate. Not all students reported were eligible for placement in the special classes. Those ineligible included children with intelligence quotients between 75-85, children with average intelligence who could not read, and retarded adolescents with social adjustment problems. Only about one of every three children referred was admitted to the ungraded classes. Others were sent back to the regular class with suggestions regarding food, and physical welfare, and their progress was monitored. Some children were sent to classes for the physically handicapped or to truant/probationary schools.

Not every parent whose child was referred and qualified for the ungraded classes was grateful for the intervention.

Still other children were rejected by the Psycho-Educational Clinic as institutional cases. Elizabeth found that "...there was a small percentage...so far below normal that they do not respond to any method of advised training," and she proposed that the Board of Education enter into an agreement with the trustees of the Syracuse Institution for the commitment of these children.

Not every parent whose child was referred and qualified for the ungraded classes was grateful for the intervention, however. At least one parent, Samuel Kastenburg of the Bronx, appealed to the magistrate in an effort to have his 11-year-old daughter removed from her ungraded class and returned to her original regular class. The magistrate, however, supported Elizabeth in her placement decision, saying that she had "supervision over ungraded classes and was qualified to decide whether children were normal or not."

CHAPTER SIX:

Elizabeth's Programs Come Under Attack

❧

Funding of Special Education Programs Criticized

While some viewed Elizabeth's Department of Ungraded Classes as a success, others, especially those on the Board of Estimates and Apportionment, the city department responsible for budgetary and financial concerns, viewed her expanding program with ever-increasing disdain. Considered an outgrowth of Superintendent Maxwell's drive to expand the school system's social agenda, the Board of Estimates looked for ways to rein in the growing school budget. Their sentiments were expressed

> *Considered an outgrowth of Superintendent Maxwell's drive to expand the school system's social agenda, the Board of Estimates looked for ways to rein in the growing school budget.*

clearly in an article published by the *New York Times* in 1906, which stated, "These special classes are regarded as a most interesting experiment in modern education...They are the conception of Superintendent Maxwell, and for this reason are regarded as another of his so-called fads and frills for which he campaigns."

In response to this attack, Maxwell stated that:

> ... this great work for suffering humanity is an outgrowth of the modern spirit of social service. No longer can it be maintained that education at the public expense is to be directed solely to secure 'the survival of the fittest' or even of the fit. One of the prime checks of public education is to develop each child, fit or unfit, to his highest capacity, as far as conditions will permit, for the work and enjoyment of life. Education cannot perform miracles, but it can lighten the burdens of the defective by engendering habits that make for right living, and by training the capacity, no matter how slight it may naturally be, for work.

Elizabeth, greatly influenced by her settlement colleagues, agreed with Maxwell that schools had a responsibility to assist children in reaching their potential, saying:

> The function of the school is to provide an environment in which the abilities and capacities of each individual may unfold and develop in a manner that will secure his maximum social efficiency. To secure this right environment, we must know the strength and the weakness of the individual's native endowment and we must know its modifications due to his experience. With these facts determined, the school life of the child will be tempered. The environment which society created for the education of the young will be so organized as to prevent in the vast majority of

cases the development of the problems of retardation, truancy and conduct disorders, and will insure to all the children the opportunity to succeed, to control and to accomplish.

Goddard Versus Farrell: Intelligence Testing and the Assessment Process

In 1912, after a decade-long battle of wills, the Board of Estimates and Apportionment asked Henry Herbert Goddard, the Director of Psychological Research at the Vineland Training School for Feeble-Minded Boys and Girls, to evaluate Elizabeth's program of ungraded

classes. While Goddard's primary charge at Vineland was to conduct research that might lead to the causes of feeble-mindedness*, he was intensely interested in the use of intelligence testing in schools. In 1910 Goddard arranged for the Binet-Simon Intelligence Test to be

"One of the prime checks of public education is to develop each child, fit or unfit, to his highest capacity, as far as conditions will permit, for the work and enjoyment of life."
-Superintendent Maxwell

* see glossary

translated for use in the United States and wanted to experiment with it on a large population of school children. Based on Goddard's perceived expertise in the education of the feeble-minded and the use of intelligence tests, the Board of Estimates anticipated a scathing rebuke of Maxwell's and Elizabeth's attempts to provide for those with low mentality. The results contained in Goddard's report, *The New York School Inquiry of 1911-1912*, surprised the sponsoring members of the Board of Estimates.

In 1910, Goddard arranged for the Binet-Simon Intelligence Test to be translated for use in the United States and wanted to experiment with it on a large population of school children.

Goddard's report was, indeed, highly critical of the ungraded class program, but not for the reasons the Board of Estimates had anticipated. While noting a steady increase in the number of ungraded classes, from 14 in 1906 to 131 in 1911-1912, with approximately 2,500 students enrolled, Goddard believed there were thousands of feeble-minded children that teachers failed to recognize. Generalizing data from an earlier New Jersey school survey, Goddard stated that:

> ... the most extensive study ever made of the children of an entire public school system of two thousand...has shown that two per cent of such children are so mentally defective as to preclude any possibility of their ever being made normal and able to take care of themselves as adults.

Goddard thus concluded that New York should be providing for at least 15,000 students in the ungraded program. Rather than suggesting an abolishment of the program as the Board of Estimates had hoped, he instead encouraged its enlargement.

Goddard went on to state that the ungraded class program was plagued by misdiagnosis, with the wrong children placed in special classes. Using Binet's intelligence tests and relying on language considered grossly offensive by today's standards, he stated that he found mentality ranging from a 3-year-old to that of a normal child, as well as "...imbeciles of Mongolian type, microcephalic idiots, hydrocephalic cases, cretins..." and "... a large number of middle and high grade imbeciles." Goddard further found "children who are really almost normal" and blamed teachers who had "misread only temporary or individual idiosyncrasies as signs of mental impairment."

Goddard Criticizes Special Education Teachers and Curriculum

Goddard's report also stated that the program needed more supervisors and better-trained, skilled teachers, something Elizabeth had already been saying for several years. Goddard went a step further, however, stating that the special class teachers were "...painfully aware of their own lack of training and their own ability to do for the child what they feel must be done." Without institutional training Goddard concluded they were "left as the physician would be who has gone through his medical course but has had no laboratory or hospital experience."

Disagreeing with those who believed that "salvation lies in the ability to read books, to write letters, and to count millions," Goddard reported that a new curriculum was needed. He wanted the schools to surrender their attempts to teach the three R's and follow the institutions' lead with a curriculum focused on manual training, arguing that the feeble-minded should be taught that which is necessary "to make life pleasanter for them...such as the training of games, of athletics, of doing things." This was, perhaps, at the heart of Goddard's report—the premise that the institution ought to be the laboratory for special classes. It is important to note that Goddard worked closely under Vineland director E. R. Johnstone who supported the ungraded classes but saw them mainly as a "clearinghouse," stating, "Keep them in special classes until they become too old for further care and they must be sent to institutions for safety."

> *This was, perhaps, at the heart of Goddard's report - the premise that the institution ought to be the laboratory for special classes.*

Farrell and Maxwell Strike Back

The report sparked both controversy and protest. Superintendent Maxwell, feeling provoked by the Board of Estimates, and wanting to rebut, faulted Goddard's logic in reaching the conclusion that the ungraded class program should be providing services to so many children, replying skeptically: "After testing 268 children...reaches the conclusion that 15,000...are mentally defective."

Elizabeth, like Maxwell, was outraged, and she attacked Goddard's survey results. In the

> *She further attacked Goddard's report, questioning mental tests as the only diagnostic tool.*

Fifteenth Annual Report (1912-1913), Elizabeth criticized Goddard for faulty research methods and questioned his sampling, noting that only 7 out of a possible 496 elementary schools were visited and only 1 out of 21 possible high schools were visited, with all of the schools located in either the Upper West Side, Lower East Side, Flushing, or the borough of Brooklyn. In her rebuttal to Goddard's report, she stated:

> It is then on a real basis of 120 observations out of a possible 750,000 that the statement is made...With these great sections of the school population left out and with a lack of definiteness as to localities that were examined, it is obvious that the distribution of children tested throughout the city was not such as would permit of fair and adequate notions of the whole school population to be obtained...It is questionable whether the 'samplings' were sufficiently distributed throughout the city and within the grades...It is obvious that with no information given as to the types of children tested, their ages, and their nationalities, no tabulations as to the times given to each examination, and the method of checking up the results, the statement of the School Inquiry Committee that two per cent of New York City public school children are feeble-minded has not been proved.

Elizabeth also challenged Goddard's belief about the relationship between the institution and the special classes. While Goddard stressed the similarities between the ungraded classes and the institutions, she saw her role as "...emphasizing the points of resemblance and minimizing the differences between the regular grade child and the ungraded class child," articulating an early vision of an argument which

> *...she saw her role as "emphasizing the points of resemblance and minimizing the differences between the regular grade child and the ungraded class child," articulating an early version of the mainstreaming debate.*

would reemerge decades later in the mainstreaming debate. She believed the goal of the special classes was to return students back to the regular classes, and therefore, the curriculum must not only teach the three R's but address diverse abilities and needs.

She further attacked Goddard's report, questioning mental tests as the only diagnostic tool stating, "...there is no universal belief in the Binet tests as the means of diagnosing deviating or exceptional mentality." Elizabeth obviously had concerns about the potential reliance on intelligence testing, noting that:

> ... from American students we learn that scholastic and other attainments and not native ability are tested by the Binet-Simon tests...the Binet-Simon tests do not properly classify children for definite treatment or for detailed care and they are not infallible in determining the mental grade of a child.

Criticizing him as a "research student in psychology," Elizabeth concluded that Goddard's report "...lacks perspective," stating it was "concerned with conditions found at a given time, but lays no stress on the circumstances which brought them about nor on those in process of correcting them..." Elizabeth continued:

> The service given by Rousseau to general education, by Pestalozzi to the education of poor children, by Horace Mann to public education in the United States, is similar to that expected from Dr. Goddard for the education of mentally defective children when he was employed by the School Inquiry Committee to investigate the aim, methods, and results of ungraded class work. To be unable to see the forest for the trees is sad. To have missed the vision is sadder still.

Final Decisions:
Intelligence Testing Loses the Battle but Wins the War

Elizabeth's sharp reply surprised Goddard. She had presented him with his first serious opposition, effectively countering his conceptualization of the relationship between institutions and the public school, and challenging his claims of expertise. By 1913 Goddard's report and Elizabeth's reply had reached the Board of Estimates and Apportionment. The Board appointed separate committees to review both reports and submit recommendations. In 1914 the committee

New Jersey's Vineland Training School. Goddard had a captive audience in the teachers who were in attendance at the summer teacher education programs sponsored by the school. The intelligence testing movement was not introduced by the Board of Education, but by teachers who were Vineland Training School graduates.

reviewing Goddard's report suggested a compromise, endorsing some of Goddard's conclusions and some of Elizabeth's. The committee agreed with Goddard's recommendations for increased salary bonuses for ungraded class teachers, leave time for additional training, and more program personnel. It rejected, however, Goddard's statements regarding the high number of potentially feeble-minded children the New York School System should expect to serve, choosing instead to endorse Elizabeth's argument that

Elizabeth obviously had concerns about the potential reliance on intelligence testing.

such a number was unproven. The committee further rebutted Goddard's claims regarding curriculum. Most importantly, however, the committee chose not to endorse Goddard's beliefs regarding intelligence testing, refusing to adopt it as the main determination for placement in the ungraded classes. In May of 1914 the recommendations reached by the committees were adopted by the Board of Education, effectively ending the debate.

Elizabeth's outrage over the reliance upon intelligence testing could do little to stem the tide, however. Despite the Board of Education's refusal to officially endorse intelligence testing, the use of intelligence tests by Goddard in the New York City Schools further served to legitimize them. Additionally, Goddard had a captive audience in the teachers who were in attendance at the summer teacher education programs sponsored by the Vineland Training School. By 1914 the movement had gained a foothold in schools, introduced not by the Board of Education but by teachers who were Vineland Training School graduates.

Changes in the Superintendence

Throughout this embattled period, Superintendent Maxwell publicly supported Elizabeth's decisions as she fought to increase the size of the Department of Ungraded Classes and further clarify its mission. After being given repeated periods of leave, however, in 1917 Maxwell was forced to resign due to illness.

Numerous figures within the New York School System and beyond applied to be Maxwell's permanent replacement. Among them were

Associate Superintendents Edward B. Shallow, John Tildsley, and William L. Ettinger (Elizabeth's former principal at Public School Number One); Board of Examiner members Jerome O'Connell and James C. Brynes; Principal John H. Denbigh; New York State Commissioner of Education John H. Finley; and Superintendent of the Los Angeles School System, Albert Shiels. After learning of a desire by New York Mayor John F. Hylan not to have an "outside expert," the Board of Education, in a secret session in May 1918, elected William L. Ettinger.

Ettinger's election must have brought a sigh of relief to Elizabeth and others involved in the ungraded classes. In a letter to *Ungraded*, a professional journal published by the Ungraded Classroom Teachers Association, dated September 6, 1918, Ettinger renewed his support for the ungraded classes and discussed his work with Elizabeth in the early stages of its development:

> My deep interest in your subject is proven by the fact that I had the privilege of cooperating with Miss Farrell in organizing in this city the first class for atypical children...We have too long assumed that all children are about alike in terms of interest and abilities.

Ettinger's support no doubt allowed Elizabeth to focus on other important issues she faced as Inspector of the Ungraded Classes.

CHAPTER SEVEN

The Immigrant-Special Education Connection

Ethnicity as a Peg for Mental Defectiveness

While Elizabeth's rebuttal of Goddard's claims may have prevented the New York City Board of Education from endorsing all of his ideas, she did not have the luxury of completely disregarding his work. In 1912, the same year as the New York School Inquiry, Goddard authored *The Kallikak Family: A Study in the Heredity of Feeble-Mindedness*, centered around data collected on a girl in residence at the Vineland Training School. Working with research assistant Elizabeth Kite, Goddard claimed to have traced the young girl's relatives, finding mental defectiveness present at every level, and concluding, therefore, it must be passed through hereditary material:

> ...The surprise and horror of it all was that no matter where we traced them, whether in the prosperous rural district, in the city slums to which some had drifted, or in the more remote mountain regions, or whether it was a question of the second or fifth generation, an appalling amount of defectiveness was everywhere found...about 65 per cent of these children have the hereditary trait...

Goddard went on to gather intelligence test data on immigrants entering the United States through Ellis Island. Based on this work, Goddard further concluded that most immigrants entering the United States were of low intelligence. He rejected the idea that the tests might be biased or that there might be physical or psychological factors influencing the results. Goddard maintained that intelligence testing "worked equally well with any child...it was, therefore, unnecessary to analyze any other variables."

> *Ayres and Gullick concluded that boys exhibited a higher percentage of retardation than girls. The lowest percentage of retardation was found in Germans, the highest percentage of retardation was found in Italians.*

The New York City Schools further reinforced Goddard's claims about immigrants when the results of an investigation on retardation were released. *Laggards in Our Schools*, conducted by Leonard P. Ayres, the former superintendent of the Puerto Rican schools, and a statistician and economist with the Sage Foundation, and Dr. Luther H. Gullick of the New York City Schools' Physical Training Department, was the first scientific inquiry into the cause of retardation. Based on information from 15 schools in New York City, including 20,000 students in Manhattan alone, Ayres and Gullick concluded that boys exhibited a higher percentage of retardation than girls. The lowest percentage of retardation was found in Germans, the highest percentage of retardation was found in Italians.

Goddard went on to gather intelligence test data on immigrants entering the United States through Ellis Island. Based on this work, Goddard further concluded that most immigrants entering the United States were of low intelligence.

Limiting Immigration

By 1911 the Commissioner of Immigration at the Port of New York had taken up the matter of feeble-minded immigrants with the Board of Education. The Board, in response, and probably with Elizabeth's assistance, furnished the Commissioner a list of foreign-born children unable to do the work because of mental defect. Immigration authorities began investigating these cases since the feeble-minded were included within a class of persons not eligible for admission to the United States and were subject to deportation if inadvertently admitted. Further, it was required they be deported if they become public charges within 3 years of admission.

The federal government, through the Ellis Island immigration authority, sought to prohibit the feeble-minded from entering the country by requiring intelligence tests of those suspected of being of low mentality. Reports of Goddard's research contributed to the passage of the Immigration Restriction Act of 1924 and the increased deportation of immigrants for reasons of mental deficiency. The act, which remained in effect until 1965, placed the heaviest restrictions on eastern and southern Europeans—Italians, Jews, Russians, and Hungarians—national groups Goddard, in his research, found to be feeble-minded.

> *...the Immigration Restriction Act of 1924...placed the heaviest restrictions on eastern and southern Europeans — Italians, Jews, Russians, and Hungarians — national groups Goddard, in his research, found to be feeble-minded.*

Elizabeth's Views on Ethnicity

These findings hit close to home for Elizabeth. During a time when there was significant concern regarding the extraordinary number of over-age or retarded children in the grades and more and more immigrant children were being referred to the ungraded classes, she could not ignore research that suggested a correlation between ethnic origin and intelligence. Disregarding her own immigrant background, she noted that "marked abilities, as well as marked disabilities, may be explained only by referring to ancestry and home." In that same report, only one year after assuming the mantle of inspector, making remarks we would consider abhorrent today, Elizabeth discussed how a child's nationality might influence referral for placement in the ungraded classes:

> The question of nationality is of very great importance. For one not familiar with national characteristics, it is an easy thing to take the heavy, sluggish response of the Slavic child as indicative of real mental inability, while children of Latin Europe, with their lively shifting and seemingly inconsistent attention to school duties, seem to the teacher to be unfitted for regular grade work...The Slav, in his native home, spends his life wresting from an unproductive soil a bare existence for self and family. He never has had leisure for that side of life which demands the nice co-ordinations, the fine muscular adjustments and quick perceptions which are demanded in our schools. The Italian, on the other hand, in the warmth, bounty, and beauty of Southern Europe, has had time all through the ages to give to things other than those concerned in keeping body and soul together. The abundance which surrounded him encouraged him to flit from one thing to the next. He could pick and choose. Today we have the Italian child in school indulging the same desire. He goes from one thing to the next until we of a different ancestry say, 'His lack of concentration is a morbid condition.'

Elizabeth Vacillates

It appears, however, that Elizabeth may have had conflicting feelings about the weight given solely to nationality, as she made contradictory statements regarding the correlation between heredity and intelligence. In her appendix to the 1909 *Annual Report to the Board of Education*, Elizabeth recalled that the last annual report of the New York State Lunacy Commission called attention to the "...alarming increase of insanity among the immigrant population." She cautioned, however, that there may be extenuating circumstances: the selection of children who were abnormally slow was more likely to be made in schools in which there were large numbers of foreign-born children or children of foreign-born parents, concluding that "schools in such neighborhoods are crowded

> *...she vacillated between accepting the "science" that correlated the two variables and rejecting the arguments wholeheartedly.*

as a rule and the exceptional child must be removed from the regular class in order to make conditions bearable at all." With this remark, Elizabeth seemed more willing to attribute retardation and feeble-mindedness to issues other than heredity.

The next year, however, Elizabeth appeared to reverse course again. In her 1910-1911 *Report on Work for Mentally Defective Children*, she quoted the writings of A. F. Tredgold, an English neurologist and author, who believed that the causes of mental deficiency fell into two categories: "morbid heredity, where some ancestral, pathological condition modifies the parental germoplasm before conception of the child," and "adverse environment, where some external factor (disease or injury) affects the embryo in the uterus, the babe at birth or the growing child after birth." She further quotes Tredgold as saying that "90 per cent of all cases of mental deficiency are due to morbid heredity," seemingly agreeing that heredity is the larger issue of concern.

The statements Elizabeth made regarding heredity and intelligence during her tenure as Inspector of the Department of Ungraded Classes are in many ways inconsistent. It appears she vacillated between accepting the "science" that correlated the two variables and rejecting the arguments wholeheartedly. One can assume a variety of circumstances were at play in her personal and professional life which may have influenced her acknowledgment of such a correlation, including her own immigrant history, the Progressive philosophy of the Henry Street Settlement and its residents, and the research considered "best science" at the time, as well as her own observations of the population being referred to and placed in the ungraded classes.

ELIZABETH FARRELL AND THE HISTORY OF SPECIAL EDUCATION

CHAPTER EIGHT:

Passing the Torch: Recruiting and Training Special Education Teachers

Finding Qualified Teachers

In 1906, when Elizabeth became Inspector of the Ungraded Department, there were only 14 classes. Fifteen years later there were over 250. Every year the number of ungraded classes throughout the school district grew. The next step, in following the long-range vision of developing a special education program, required Elizabeth to move away from class work and into teacher development.

In her role as Inspector of the Department of Ungraded Classes, Elizabeth Farrell faced many of the same issues that special education directors deal with today. Perhaps most critical among them was the shortage of qualified teachers to meet the demands for the number of ungraded classes required in the public schools throughout New York City. As head of the department it was considered one of Elizabeth's chief duties to discover those teachers who had a natural aptitude for dealing with atypical children. It was no easy task.

Elizabeth Farrell faced many of the same issues that special education directors deal with today. Perhaps most critical among them was the shortage of qualified special education teachers

Qualifications

To assist Elizabeth in procuring additional ungraded teachers, the Board of Examiners began to conduct competitive examinations. These exams were open to women with at least 3 years teaching experience, as well as teachers in private schools and school districts outside of New York City. The examination consisted of three parts: written, oral, and practical. The written portion included two papers, one on the methods of ungraded instruction and the other on principles of education. The practical exam consisted of skill demonstration in such areas as basketry, piano playing, drawing, and sewing; and the oral exam required the candidate to be put in charge of an ungraded class in order to observe her use of the English language and her classroom management ability. If the applicant did not hold a regular license to teach in the New York City public school system, a certificate of physical fitness, along with proof of vaccinations and citizenship, was required.

Methods of Recruitment

For the most part, however, Elizabeth was forced to resort to less than ideal methods to secure teachers for ungraded classes. One of these was to ask for volunteers among the already licensed teachers employed within the school system. On occasion, a teacher would volunteer because of a real interest in helping struggling children. Oftentimes, though, teachers would volunteer because those

Elizabeth was in favor of increased salaries for ungraded class teachers... believing they rendered a valuable service and that the salaries were not commensurate with their difficult work.

employed in the special classes made between $1,900 and $3,250 per year, an increase in salary over regular class teachers.

Despite this, Elizabeth was in favor of increased salaries for ungraded class teachers, believing they rendered a valuable service and that the salaries were not commensurate with their difficult work. She felt that substantial increases might induce larger numbers of teachers to prepare themselves for a career in the ungraded classes.

If no regularly licensed teachers volunteered, administrators sometimes chose teachers who were about to retire and might be looking to
escape the rigid inspections given to work in the regular grades.
Administrators also frequently turned to teachers who had a genuine
ability to discipline a class, believing they might be well suited for
ungraded class work.

Training Special Education Teachers

Compounding the difficulty that Elizabeth faced in recruiting teachers was that these teachers needed special training, and there were few
programs in the area able to provide adequate instruction in the methods
of teaching defective children. One of these institutional training programs took place at the Vineland Training School for Feeble-Minded
Girls and Boys. This program was run by E. R. Johnstone and
Elizabeth's old rival, Henry Herbert Goddard. Johnstone, Vineland's
superintendent, advocated "education in special classes until sexual
maturity, to be followed by locally funded municipal custodial industrial
institutions in the cities and by rural colonies to reclaim waste land."

The second program, offered during the school year through
Teachers College, was perhaps one of the best known and more cohesive
with Elizabeth's programming ideas since she served as an instructor,
but it required teachers to travel miles after the school day had ended. In

her *Thirteenth Annual Report* (1910-1911), Farrell commented on the burden placed upon those who chose to become ungraded class teachers:

> Upon investigation, it was found that one teacher who took up ungraded work spent $150 and for five years has taken three hours a week in one of the local colleges. To take only the specialized work on the subject which was offered in the city necessitated miles of travel after the school day was over. This outlay of money and strength many good teachers are unable to make.

The First School for Special Educators– The Brooklyn Training School

In 1906 the Board of Education led by Superintendent Maxwell attempted to address this thorny issue, passing a by-law concerning ungraded teacher training. It authorized 3 months' leave with full pay for ungraded teachers to study in a school that trained teachers of defectives. Elizabeth, however, felt that while this was a good first step, it didn't alleviate the burden on ungraded teachers, their families, or the department, and she proposed establishing a 3-month graduate course at the Brooklyn Training School for teachers assigned to ungraded classes, possibly because she could design it to specifically coordinate with New York City's ungraded class program.

Although originally not put into operation due to a lack of funds, in 1912 the idea was adopted by the Board of Education. Fifteen teachers were selected to attend the Brooklyn Training School in cohort groups.

The first group of ungraded teachers reported in November of that year, with the second group beginning the course of study the following April. Teachers selected for cohort groups came from two areas: the first group held a regular teaching license and had three years' successful teaching experience in regular grades. These teachers were assigned to teach in ungraded classes with the appropriate salary for two years, at the end of which, they must have taken the exam and obtained an ungraded teaching license. The majority of the teachers enrolled in the Brooklyn Training School's graduate course were secured by this method. The second group of teachers was appointed from eligible lists as the result of ungraded teacher examinations. They had to be over 21 years old but less than 46 and meet all the academic, professional, and special qualifications required in the Board of Education by-laws.

The teachers attended classes organized to provide key information on the education of mentally defective children and the development of those skills necessary to be an ungraded class teacher, including psychology, physiology, class management, and manual training. In her *Report on Work for Mentally Defective Children* (1912-1913), Elizabeth described some of the courses:

> **Psychology**: The course will aim to give a knowledge of the nature and the activity of mind from the standpoint of normal development... Pathological conditions of attention, memory, will, etc. will be analyzed...

Physiology: ...Abnormalities and pathological conditions found in school children will be studied and their relation to normal mental development demonstrated...

Methods: ...Attention will be called to the necessity of establishing correct fundamental or primary habits—hence the obligation to present the concrete rather than the abstract, materials rather than symbols in the beginning work...

During the course of study, the Brooklyn Training School teachers also worked in ungraded classrooms under the supervision of Elizabeth or one of her assistant inspectors. Ungraded class teachers were observed and evaluated, and observations were followed up with a conference. In this 1 and a half hour meeting, both strong and weak teaching areas were identified and means of improvement discussed.

Eventually, the course of study at the Brooklyn Training School was extended to three years, and the curriculum was differentiated to identify those teachers who seemed best suited to teach the elementary, middle, or upper grades, classifying students according to their ability. Growth in the number of program applicants may have allowed the Board of Education to create more stringent requirements, yet the program proved such a success in securing qualified teachers that Elizabeth recommended that similar programs be established in other parts of the city.

Professional Development Teacher Forums

As Inspector of the Ungraded Department, Elizabeth sought ways to encourage professional growth among its members. Once employed, ungraded teachers were assigned to a small group for a 2-year period. These groups, which included experienced teachers, met monthly so they could, in Elizabeth's words "...develop the technique for remedial work in their classes." As part of these groups, they gave demonstrations, formulated supply lists, participated in discussions, and examined problems related to health education, practical applications for math, manual training, industrial, household, and fine arts, and the practical and economical use of industrial supplies.

> *...Elizabeth sought ways to encourage professional growth...*

Ungraded teachers also participated in periodic meetings with psychologists from agencies involved with ungraded classes in which they would discuss articles in professional periodicals and exchange views regarding psychological materials and evaluation procedures.

Elizabeth also worked to improve the ungraded teaching profession through the publication of *Ungraded* magazine, a professional periodical sponsored by the Ungraded Classroom Teachers Association. At its inception in May of 1915, Elizabeth participated as a member of the magazine's advisory board. Later she became more involved, taking first the position of Associate Editor with, among others, Elizabeth A. Walsh, her assistant, and later assuming the position of editor, authoring such articles as "The Backward Child" (1915), "The Unclassified Child"

(1923), "Mental Hygiene Problems of Maladjusted Children"(1924), and "What New York City Does for Its Problem Children" (1925). She also used the magazine as a vehicle to publish research conducted in the ungraded classes, submitting "Preliminary Report on Children Discharged from Ungraded Classes" (1915), and "Survey of Nationality of Children in Ungraded Classes" (1921). It was her relationship with *Ungraded* and the Ungraded Classroom Teachers Association that provided her with a platform to showcase her views regarding special children and their unique needs in the classroom.

University Work in Teacher Education

Elizabeth's work to foster professional growth was not confined to her department, however. She spent numerous years working to educate students at the university level. In 1906, she was awarded a Bachelor of Science degree from New York University, and was later invited to work as a lecturer in the School of Pedagogy. Employed at New York University from 1913-1916, Elizabeth taught four courses related to the supervision and instruction of special classes: Observation and Practice, where students had the opportunity to observe special classes and participate in readings, discussions, and lectures; Observation and Practice—Advanced Course, where students continued the observation work begun in the earlier course; Organization and Management of Special Classes, which covered the principles and practices of the special classes and discussed factors regarding growth, supervision, and classification; and Standards for Measuring Instruction, where a student taught a group of children and had their work observed and discussed.

Elizabeth also served as a lecturer at Teachers College, Columbia University, from 1915 until her death in 1932, teaching several classes jointly with her colleague, Dr. Leta S. Hollingworth, a professor of educational psychology and chief of the psychological lab at Bellevue Hospital. Together, they taught and supervised advanced students in graduate courses who conducted investigations or experiments in the special classes. These graduate courses included Methods of Teaching in Special Classes, where Elizabeth reviewed the methods and subject matter of the elementary school needed by the special child as well as the diagnosis of failure; and Supervision of Special Classes, which was designed for students who planned on becoming principals, supervisors, instructors, or supervisory officers in teacher training schools.

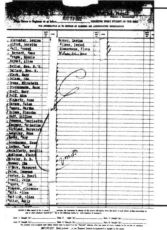

Class roster for course taught by Elizabeth Farrell at Columbia University - signed with her initial.

CHAPTER NINE

Elizabeth Works to Establish Special Education Professional Organizations

The American Psychological Association

In addition to developing training programs for special education teachers, Elizabeth wanted to promote collegial relationships and communication among those who worked with special needs children. Seeking to recognize the looming impact that the field of applied psychology and intelligence testing would have on the placement of children in ungraded classes, she and several others who worked in education became members of the American Psychological Association (APA). As the number of applied psychologists grew, they looked to the APA for leadership. However, at that time the American Psychological Association was still strongly committed to the scientific side of psychology. To meet what they believed to be a growing need, Farrell, her assistant, Elizabeth A. Walsh, and Dr. Leta S. Hollingworth of Teachers College, attempted to organize the New York State Association of Consulting Psychologists at a meeting of the American Psychological Association in 1916. Unfortunately, due to the APA's lack of interest, the new organization didn't gain momentum.

Years later the organization resurfaced. In 1921, under the leadership of psychologist and Rutgers professor David Mitchell, the New York State Association of Consulting Psychologists (later the New York State Psychological Association) became the first state level psychological association as well as the first to advocate for the recognition of the profession of psychology. Organized, according to The Psychological Bulletin, for the purposes of "the promotion of high standards of professional qualifications for consulting psychologists" and to "stimulate research work in the field of psychological analysis and evaluation," membership was limited to those who had a minimum requirement of two years' graduate work in psychology. This new organization, the New York State Association of Consulting Psychologists, valued applied psychology at a time when the American Psychological Association's emphasis was on research. At that formative time, the organization's executive committee included Mitchell as president, Elizabeth A. Walsh as secretary-treasurer, Farrell, and Hollingworth.

...Elizabeth wanted to promote collegial relationships and communication among those who worked with special needs children.

Perhaps the organization's biggest accomplishment during those early years was the June 1922 publication of a pamphlet by the American Red Cross entitled *Examination of Pre-School Age Children: Examination of Children Upon Registering Before Entering School*. The pamphlet, detailing mental test data on 1,113 children entering grades kindergarten and 1A in eight New York City public schools, was created in cooperation with Farrell and the Department of Ungraded Classes in June 1921. The goal of the publication was to provide data for principals to use in classifying children for the ungraded classes. It was believed that if all examinations could be made in June, physical defects could be corrected during the summer through the coordination of services of the school nurses and the American Red Cross, eliminating the interruption of school attendance by first–year students. In this venture, Elizabeth used her involvement in the New York State Association of Consulting Psychologists to ease the burden on her Department of Ungraded Classes by lessening the number of children referred to the Psycho-Educational Clinic once the school year began.

The National Education Association

Elizabeth was also involved at the ground floor in organizations focused on teaching special needs children. In 1897, upon petition of Alexander Graham Bell, the Department of Special Education of the National Education Association (NEA) was formed. In 1911 Elizabeth became vice-president of the organization, and later went on to become president in 1916 or 1918 (accounts vary). It

> *In 1897, upon petition of Alexander Graham Bell, the Department of Special Education of the National Education Association (NEA) was formed.*

was in this leadership capacity that she promoted collegiality, bringing together individuals representing day and residential schools, clinics, private agencies, state departments of education, hospitals, and universities to discuss topics related to special needs. Unfortunately, records indicate that the department disintegrated in 1918 due to a lack of publications, meager committee work, and limited funds.

Meeting at the George Washington University for the national Council for the Education of Exceptional Children under the NEA convention

The Council for Exceptional Children

After the dissolution of the NEA's Department of Special Education, an organization was needed that would fill its void and keep special class teachers in touch with each other and with developments in the field. Farrell was teaching summer courses at Teachers College in August of 1922 when a group of students enrolled in her courses, led by Henrietta Johnson of Oakland, California, asked her to attend a meeting to discuss possible ways to promote fellowship among educators as well as a means of exchanging ideas among workers in special education. At

Plaque at CEC Headquarters
Arlington, VA

that meeting, the International Council for the Education of Exceptional Children (later the Council for Exceptional Children - CEC) was formed, and Farrell, known for stressing the importance of communication among professionals, was unanimously elected president.

At that first organizational meeting, the Council adopted three aims: to unite those interested in educational problems of "special children," to emphasize the education of "special children" rather than his/her identification, and to establish professional standards for teachers in the field of special education. Membership was open to any person who was interested in the education of exceptional children, and dues were $1 per year.

The Council, originally affiliated with the National Education Association, held meetings at the same time and place as the NEA's Department of Superintendence until the affiliation was withdrawn in 1977. At the first annual meeting of the International Council in 1922, Elizabeth spoke about the purpose of such a teaching organization and the responsibilities of those who were called to join:

The International Council for the Education of Exceptional Children will be the clearinghouse of knowledge useful to teachers in their special fields. The Council will be for teachers the authoritative body on questions of subject matter, method and school or class organization. At its annual meeting it hopes to present ideas proved to be useful in the training of exceptional children. The Council hopes to stimulate the teaching of children at least to the extent that psychologists have stimulated classification on the basis of intellectual power. The Council will stand back of its membership in demanding high professional qualifications for those designated to serve in its fields. It will demand freedom for its members as practitioners. It will promote the idea that educational work, whether in institutions or in public day schools, must be in the hands of and directed by men and women trained in the science and art of education...With modesty and great humility all its members accept responsibilities of their calling. They hope that because of their efforts public education in this country will be less machine-made and more individual; that the schools of this country will use the ability of each pupil group to its maximum; that the school will fit its burden to the back which bears it; that it will bring the opportunity of successful achievement to every child.

Several items of importance were included in meeting discussions throughout the years, including teacher training, professional collegiality, and program and instructional design. In 1924, at the second annual meeting of the Council, a new section of the professional journal *Ungraded*, of which Elizabeth was editor, was designated to serve as the official pronouncement of the council, thus linking the journal, the Ungraded Classroom Teacher's Association, and the Council together.

At the fourth annual meeting in 1926, Farrell stepped down as president of the Council, taking instead the position of vice-president. By then there were over 400 members in the organization, with members from 33 states, the District of Columbia, Canada, India, and Holland, reflecting perhaps both the need for such an organization as well as Elizabeth's strength in fostering its growth.

> *...in 1926...there were over 400 members in the organization, with members from 33 states, the District of Columbia, Canada, India, and Holland, reflecting perhaps both the need for such an organization as well as Elizabeth's strength in fostering its growth.*

In 1929, at the Council's seventh annual meeting, a tribute was read to Elizabeth for her years of service to the Council and her contributions in the field of education and she was awarded lifetime membership. At its tenth annual meeting in 1932, a resolution was passed noting Farrell's silver anniversary with the Department of Ungraded Classes. Following that, the Council sent her a congratulatory telegram.

Many decades later Elizabeth's leadership is still recognized among current Council members. A bronze tablet bearing her profile hangs in the offices of the Council for Exceptional Children in Arlington,

Virginia, reminding everyone about the guiding philosophies of its first president:

> In memory of Elizabeth Farrell, pioneer teacher of backward children in New York City. She devoted her life to the development of the ungraded classes and left to all children in need of special help the assurance that they might find it in the public schools.

CHAPTER TEN:

End of a Career

ଓଃ

Recognition

Elizabeth celebrated the 25th anniversary of the Ungraded Class Department in March of 1932 with a party held at the Hotel Astor in New York. A variety of people spoke, including Dr. John H. Finley from the Department of Education; Dr. William H. Ettinger, Elizabeth's principal at the Henry Street School and superintendent of the New York Public School System; Lillian Wald of the Henry Street Settlement; Charles C. Burlingham, former president of the Board of Education; and Dr. Leta S. Hollingworth of Teachers College. She also received congratulatory telegrams from numerous influential people familiar with her work, among them Warden Lewis E. Lawes of Ossining "Sing Sing" Prison; Mrs. Franklin D. Roosevelt; Felix Warburg, president of the Board of Directors of the Henry Street Settlement; the International Council for the Education of Exceptional Children; and E. R. Johnstone, Director of the Vineland Training School for Feeble-Minded Girls and Boys.

Additional telegrams were received from Ray Lyman Wilbur, Secretary of the Interior, who wrote: "You have pioneered in this important field of education, and your accomplishments help to prove the sound public policy of training the handicapped child to help himself," and from Dr. F. J. Kelley of the United States Office of Education, who referred to the effect the ungraded classes had on the whole field of education when he wrote:

> It emphasizes the right of the child to be dealt with intelligently as society's charge and not as its outcast...with the result that the whole system of education has been modified to consider improved conditions for all children.

Not long after the celebration, Farrell requested a leave of absence to travel to Battle Creek, Michigan and the Cleveland Clinic, in Cleveland, Ohio for treatment of a heart ailment. Several members of her family, including her older brother George and younger sisters Ida and Agnes Irene, traveled with her.

Elizabeth Farrell passed away unexpectedly during treatment on October 15, 1932.

Her family accompanied her body back to Utica, New York, her hometown, to be buried in the family plot. Although many in Utica may not have realized the impact of her life's work, an editorial in the New York Times that ran after her death reminded everyone how important her presence had been:

> There are shrines where persons healed of their infirmities leave their crutches or other 'votive offerings' to the saint thus commemorated. If all the 'atypical,' 'handicapped,' 'ungraded,' children who had been helped by the late Miss

> Farrell, together with those who have worked with and
> under her, were to bring such symbols of their gratitude,
> additional rooms for these maladjusted little ones would be
> necessary...The moral of Miss Farrell's educational success
> is 'individualization.'

Over the next year, the loss of Elizabeth's presence was keenly felt by
her New York City community and school system. A memorial service
held in her honor in February of 1933 at the Cosmopolitan Club in New
York included many of the same speakers as the 25th anniversary cele-
bration the year before. Speakers included Dr. John H. Finley, Dr. Leta
S. Hollingworth, and Felix Warburg, as well as Dr. Edward L.
Thorndike, professor of education at Teachers College, Dr. Thomas M.
Balliet, professor emeritus at New York University, and Margaret
McCooey, associate superintendent of schools.

The president of the International Council for Exceptional Children,
I. Grace Ball, sent the following in a telegram to the memorial:

> In the passing of Elizabeth E. Farrell, the International
> Council for Exceptional Children has lost its founder, a
> wise counselor, a rare friend. For her clear vision, her
> unfailing help, her warm championship of children, espe-
> cially these handicapped little ones under her care, she will
> ever be a living influence in those whose lives she touched.
> We mourn her passing; we rejoice in her living.

In May of 1933 the faculty and students of Oswego Normal and
Training School dedicated a bronze tablet to Farrell to recognize her

contribution in establishing their Department of Special Training in 1916 and her impact on special needs education. Dr. John H. Finley wrote the inscription:

> In memory of Elizabeth Farrell, Class of 1895, Oswego State Normal and Training School, who gave her life that the least might live as abundantly as their handicaps of mind or body permitted. A teacher of the atypical, the sub-normal, the dull of spirit, the slow of speech, the inert. In teaching them she also gave instruction in the method by which the normal, the bright, and alert should be taught. Beginning with a little group of boys in the Lower East Side of Manhattan, she became the tutelary of the ungraded classes for all New York City, demanding no child too atypical to be neglected...Keep we the altars kindled. Guard we the sacred fires.

Summary

Elizabeth's Role in Special Education

Although blessed with an upbringing of education and wealth, Elizabeth E. Farrell turned her back on her family's fortune to embrace the Progressive Reform Movement and work to change the educational structure of the New York City Public School System. Laboring alongside Lillian D. Wald and others, she laid the groundwork for a curriculum designed to address the needs of those children unable to succeed in the regular class setting. Indeed, her vision for the schools was far in advance of the profession at the time, and her philosophies became the basis for special education programs in use in the United States today.

Throughout her 25 years as Inspector of the Department of Ungraded Classes, she made decisions that proved to be both significant and influential in the field of education. Legislation passed in the United States decades later, including Public Law 94-142, the Education of All Handicapped Children Act, and its reauthorization, the Individuals with Disabilities Education Act, would confirm her convictions.

It was perhaps Elizabeth's first decision as department head that would prove the most monumental for the future of special needs programming and legislative action. After extensive study of the special class program in Great Britain, she clarified her hopes for the ungraded classes, seeking to adopt a similar methodical procedure of examination and record-keeping but arguing against any attempt to copy Great

Britain's system of separate programs, separate facilities, and separate schools. Believing such a policy would stigmatize and differentiate students with special needs, she articulated an argument expressed years later in the landmark Supreme Court decision *Brown v. Board of Education* (1954), which prohibited the idea of "separate but equal."

Elizabeth also disputed the premise held by many at that time that special class programs were to serve as a precursor to institutional life. The goal of the special class, she believed, was not to prepare students for lives in the institution but to return children back to the regular class setting after their difficulties have been addressed. Again, this judgment proved pivotal, as it served as the framework for later mainstreaming efforts in this country.

Elizabeth fought the use of intelligence testing as the single measure for placement of a child in the ungraded class, going up against one of the nation's premier experts on the use of intelligence testing in the schools, Henry H. Goddard. Her strong stance on this topic effectively prevented the New York City Board of Education from endorsing Goddard's findings regarding intelligence testing in his 1911-1912 *New York School Inquiry* report.

Instead, Elizabeth supported a comprehensive referral and placement procedure based on several different measures, in the hopes that children would be more appropriately identified and placed. She anticipated types of exceptionalities that had not yet been identified, comparing the emerging science of education to the field of medicine, saying:

> There was a time in the evolution of medical science when people fell into two groups—well people and sick peo-

> ple...The tendency in medical research is to make closer
> classification in order that treatment may be more exact
> and definite. The application of a method similar to this is
> what the school needs.

To further this effort, she created the Psycho-Educational Clinic,
employing professionals from education, medicine, psychology, and
social services, to operate in conjunction with the Department of
Ungraded Classes. To this day, a variety of testing and evaluation procedures are required before a child can be placed into a program of special
education.

As Inspector, one of her chief duties was to secure teachers for the
ungraded classes, and she struggled with the shortage of qualified teachers. To help address this issue, Elizabeth taught at several universities,
among them Teachers College and New York University, attempting to
interest and encourage others to choose a career in the ungraded classes.
Once employed, she promoted their professional growth through the use
of teacher cohort groups, pairing novice and experienced teachers,
allowing them the freedom to discuss issues relevant to the ungraded
classes. She offered her guidance through the magazine *Ungraded*, published by the Ungraded Classroom Teachers Association, serving first on
its advisory board and later becoming an editor and frequent contribu-
tor.

Additionally, she forever linked the profession of psychology to
special education through her work with the New York State Association
of Consulting Psychologists (later the New York State Psychological
Association). Although not a psychologist herself, she recognized the

importance of applied psychology in the schools and sought to build a body of knowledge based on information rather than opinion. Her union with this professional organization served to increase her credibility and was yet another example of the many ways in which Elizabeth promoted collegiality and professional improvement among those that labored in the public school systems. This organization continues to thrive.

As founding president of the International Council for the Education of Exceptional Children (later the Council for Exceptional Children), Elizabeth further promoted collegiality and professionalism among those who worked with the special classes, providing the support that could only be obtained through fellowship with others in the field. The Council, which began with a group of educators taking summer courses taught by Farrell at Teachers College, has grown to become the leading professional special education organization today.

We can only speculate as to how special education in the United States would be different were it not for the dedication and labor of Elizabeth E. Farrell. Perhaps her friend and mentor Lillian D. Wald stated it best when she reflected upon the importance of Elizabeth's work:

> Looking back upon the struggles to win formal recognition of the existence of these children...we realize our colleague's devotion to them, her power to excite enthusiasm in us, and her understanding of the social implications of their existence, came from a deep-lying principle that every human being, even the least lovely, merits respectful consideration of his rights and personality.

Glossary of Early 20th Century
Special Education Terms *

<u>Atypical or atypical children</u>, refers to children who have educational needs that differ or are beyond what is usual for a child in school.[1]

<u>Defective, mental defective, or mentally deficient</u> refers to children who, for a variety of reasons, are unable to succeed in the traditional classes in the public school. The term defective is used "in lieu of 'ungraded' in some localities because of its vagueness."[2] Further, it is a general term used to describe students with "varying degree of mental defect."[3]

<u>Feeble-minded or Feeble-mindedness</u> comprises "all degrees of mental defectives due to arrested or imperfect mental development as a result of which the person affected is incapable of competing on equal terms with his normal fellows, or of managing himself or his affairs with ordinary prudence."[4]

<u>Laggard</u> refers to "the slow child, the child whose development is sluggish, one who, with other things equal, is overage for his grade."[5]

<u>Retarded</u> refers to the number of years a child is behind in his or her education. For example, a 12-year old student in the 4th grade would be 2 years retarded. It can also describe a student who is not progressing through the grades.

<u>Ungraded</u> is used to describe "one who presents a problem of special education which cannot be more adequately met elsewhere."[6]

101

<u>Ungraded class or ungraded classes</u> refers to "a class of several grades composed of children of low mentality."[7] It describes the organizational structure of special education classes in the New York City public school system. These classes contrast the traditional, age-related graded system employed in school systems. Special class or special classes refer also to this nontraditional system of organization.

*These terms would be considered grossly offensive by today's standards. However, at the turn of the previous century, they were commonly used diagnostic definitions and were considered politically correct.

1 Frequently, terms used in literature of the time were not defined; it appears their meanings were "understood." Often these terms are used interchangeably. When no definition could be located, this author created a working definition as best as could be determined by the available literature.

2 "Teachers Council Report of Committee on Special Schools and Classes. Re: Place of Ungraded Child in the Public School System," 5 November 1920. Farrell Papers, Special Collections, Milbank Memorial Library, Teachers College, New York.

3 Andrew W. Edson, "Subject: Report of Teachers' Council on Ungraded Classes," 1 April 1921. Farrell Papers, Special Collections, Milbank Memorial Library, Teachers College, New York.

4 "Teachers Council Report of Committee on Special Schools and Classes. Re: Place of Ungraded Child in the Public School System," 5 November 1920.

5 Elizabeth E. Farrell, "The Backward Child," Ungraded 1 n.1 (May 1915): 4.

6 Edson, "Subject: Report of Teachers' Council on Ungraded Classes," 1 April 1921.

7 Ibid.

Bibliography

BOOKS

Adams, A. G. (1990). An Illustrated Historical Guide With Gazetteer. New York: Fordham University Press.

Ayres, L. P. (1909). Laggards in Our Schools: A Study of Retardation and Elimination in City School Systems. New York: Charities Publications Committee.

Ball, T. S. (1971). Itard, Seguin, and Kepart: Sensory Education-A Learning Interpretation. Columbus, OH: Charles E. Merrill.

Barzum, J, & Graff, H. F. (1992). The Modern Researcher (5th ed.). New York: Harcourt Brace Jovanovich.

Batterberry, M., & Batterberry, A. (1973). On the Town in New York: A History of Eating, Drinking, and Entertainments From 1776 to the Present. New York: Charles Scribner's Sons.

Burke, P. (Ed). (1991). New Perspectives on Historical Writing. University Park, PA: Pennsylvania State University Press.

Coss, C. (1989). Lillian D. Wald: Progressive Activist. New York: The Feminist Press at the City University of New York.

Cruickshank, W. M., & Johnson, G. O. (Eds.). (1967). Education of Exceptional Children and Youth. Englewood Cliffs, NJ: Prentice-Hall.

Davis, K. C. (1995). Don't Know Much About History. New York: Avon Books.

Dushee, K. H. (1952). As You Pass By. New York: Hastings House.

Ellis, D. M., Frost, J. A., Syrett, H, C., & Carmau, H. F. (1957). A Short History of New York State. New York: Cornell University Press.

Ensign, F. C. (1969). Compulsory School Attendance and Child Labor: A Study of the Historical Development of Regulations Compelling Attendance and Limiting the Labor of Children in a Selected Group of States. New York: Arno Press.

Evers, A., Cromley, E., Blackmar, B., & Harris, N. (1979). Resorts of the Catskills. New York: St. Martin's Press.

Farrell, E. E. (1974). President's Address: First Annual Meeting of the International Council for Exceptional Children. In S. A. Kirk & F. E. Lord (Eds.), Exceptional Children: Educational Resources and Perspectives (pp. 3-9). Boston: Houghton-Mifflin.

Farrell, E. E. (1976). A Preliminary Report on the Careers of Three Hundred Fifty Children Who Have Left Ungraded Classes. In M. Rosen, G. R. Clark, & M. S. Kivitz (Eds.), The History of Mental Retardation: Collected Papers: Vol. 2. (pp. 14-21). Baltimore: University Park Press.

Goddard, H. H. (1920). Human Efficiency and Levels of Intelligence. Princeton, NJ: Princeton University Press.

Goddard, H. H. (1912). The Kallikak Family: A Study in the Heredity of Feeble-Mindedness. New York: Macmillan.

Goddard, H. H. (1919). Psychology of the Normal and Subnormal. New York: Dodd, Mead, & Co.

Gottschalk. L. (1964). Understanding History: A Primer of Historical Method. New York: Alfred A. Knopf.

Hallahan, D. P., & Kauffman, J. M. (1978). Exceptional Children: Introduction to Special Education. Englewood Cliffs, NJ: Prentice-Hall.

Hewit. F. M., & Forness, S. R. (1977). Education of Exceptional Learners (2nd ed.). Boston: Allyn & Bacon.

Hofstadter, R. (1955). The Age of Reform: From Bryan to F.D.R. New York: Alfred A. Knopf.

Hogan, J. D. (1994). A History of the New York State Psychological Association: The Early Years (First Draft). New York: St, John's University.

Itard, J. M. G. (1962). The Wild Boy of Aveyron. (G. Humphrey & M. Humphrey, Trans.). Englewood Cliffs, NJ: Prentice-Hall.

Jones, G. E. (1994). Modern Wales: A Concise History. Cambridge, England: Cambridge University Press.

Kauffman, J. M., & Hallahan, D. P. (1981). Handbook of Special Education. Englewood Cliffs, NJ: Prentice-Hall.

Kellogg, W. O. (1995). American History the Easy Way (2nd ed.). Hauppauge: Barron's Educational Series.

Kirk. S. A., & Lord, F. E. (Eds.). (1974). Exceptional Children: Educational Resources and Perspectives. Boston: Houghton-Mifflin.

Krishef, C. H. (1983). An Introduction to Mental Retardation. Springfield: Charles C. Thomas.

Lane, H. (1976). The Wild Boy of Aveyron. Cambridge, MA: Harvard University Press.

Lincoln, Y. S., & Guba. E. G. (1986). Naturalistic Inquiry. Beverly Hills: Sage.

Link, A. S., & McCormick, R. L. (1983). Progressivism. Arlington Heights, IL: Harlan Davidson.

Longstreet, S. (1975.) City on Two Rivers: Profiles on New York-Yesterday and Today. New York: Hawthorn Books.

Marks, R. (1981). The Idea of IQ. Washington, DC: University Press of America.

McCarthy, D. (1956). History of the New York State Psychological Association. Unpublished manuscript.

Peter, L. J. (1977). Peter's Quotations: Ideas for Our Time. New York: Quill.

Rogers, D. (1988). SUNY College at Oswego: Its Second Century Unfolds (1st ed.). Oswego, NY: Auxilary Services, State University College at Oswego.

Safford, P. L., & Safford, E. J. (1996). A History of Childhood and Disability. New York: Teachers College Press.

Sarason, S. B., & Doris, J. (1979). Educational Handicap, Public Policy and Social History. New York: The Free Press.

Scally, R. (1995). The Irish and the 'Famine Exodus' of 1847. The Cambridge Survey of World Migration (R. Cohen, Ed.).Cambridge, England: Cambridge University Press.

Schrier, A. (1958). Ireland and the American Emigration, 1850-1900. Minneapolis: University of Minnesota Press.

Shafer, R. J. (1974). A Guide to Historical Method (Rev. ed.). Homewood, IL: Dorsey Press.

Siegel, B. (1983). Lillian Wald of Henry Street. New York: Macmillian.

Smith, J. D. (1985). Minds Made Feeble. Rockville, MD: Aspen Systems Corporation.

Snyderman, M., & Rothman, S. (1988). The IQ Controversy, the Media and Public Policy. New Brunswick: Transition Books.

State University College of Education (Oswego, NY). (1911). History of the First Half-Century of Oswego State Normal and Training School, Oswego, New York, 1861-1911. Oswego, NY: State University College of Education.

Swift, D. W. (1971). Ideology and Change in the Public Schools: Latent Functions of Progressive Education. Columbus, OH: Merrill.

Thomson, J. H. (Ed.). (1966). Geography of New York State. Syracuse: Syracuse University Press.

Tosh, J. (1984). The Pursuit of History: Aims, Methods, and New Directions in the Study of History. New York: Longman Group Limited.

Tratter, W. I. (1999). From Poor Law to Welfare State: A History of Social Welfare in America (6th ed.). New York: The Free Press.

Wald, L. D. (1915). The House on Henry Street. New York: Henry Holt & Co.

Wald, L. D. (1941). Windows on Henry Street. Boston: Little, Brown, & Co.

Walsh, J. J. (1982). Vignettes of Old Utica. Utica, NY: Utica Public Library.

Witmer, L. (Ed.). (1914-1915). Ungraded Class Vs. Special Class. Vol. VIII, The Psychological Clinic: A Journal of Orthogenics for the Normal Development of Every Child, Appendix A. Philadelphia, PA: Psychological Clinic Press.

Wolcott, H. F. (1990). On Seeking and Rejecting Validity in Qualitative Research. In E. W. Elisnerk & A. Peshkin (Eds.), Qualitative Inquiry in Education: The Continuing Debate (pp. 121-152). New York: Teachers College.

Yans-McLaughlin, V., & Lightman, M. (1997). Ellis Island and the Peopling of America: The Official Guide. New York, The New Press.

Yssledyke, J. E., & Algozzine, B. (1982). Critical Issues in Special and Remedial Education. Boston: Houghton Mifflin.

Zenderland, L. (1998). Measuring Minds: Henry Herbert Goddard and the Origins of American Intelligence Testing. New York: Cambridge University Press.

ELIZABETH FARRELL AND THE HISTORY OF SPECIAL EDUCATION

Articles

Allington, R. L. (1994). What's Special About Special Programs for Children Who Find Learning to Read Difficult? Journal of Reading Behavior, 26, 1-21.

Annual Meeting of the International Council for the Education of Exceptional Children. (no date). Ungraded VIII, 7, 161.

Annual Meeting of the International Council for the Education of Exceptional Children. (no date). Ungraded IX, 3, 72.

Annual Meeting of the International Council for the Education of Exceptional Children. (no date). Ungraded IX, 5, 122.

Baker, H. J. (1934). Common Problems in the Education of the Normal and the Handicapped. Exceptional Children, 1, 39-40.

Brabner, G., Jr. (1967, February). The Myth of Mental Retardation. Training School Bulletin, 63, 149-152.

Court Upholds Act of Miss Farrell. (no date). Ungraded VII, 5, 117.

Doll, E. E. (1988). Before the Big Time: Early History of the Training School at Vineland, 1888-1949. American Journal on Mental Retardation, 93, 1-15.

Editorial, (September, 1918) Ungraded, 4 1.

Educational Events: In Memory of Elizabeth E. Farrell. (1932, October 29). School and Society, 36(931), 571.

Educational Events: In Memory of Elizabeth E. Farrell. (1933, March 4). School and Society, 37(949), 272.

Elizabeth E. Farrell. (1935). Exceptional Children, 1(3), 72-76.

Farrell, E. E. (1906, 1907). Special Classes in the New York City Schools. Journal of Psycho-Asthenics, 11(1-4), 91-96.

Farrell, E. E. (1915). The Backward Child. Ungraded I, 3, 4-9.

Farrell, E. E. (1915). Preliminary Report on Children Discharged From Ungraded Classes. Ungraded VI, 3, 87-89.

Farrell, E. E. (1920). Selection of Children for Psychological and Psychiatric Exam. Ungraded VI, 2.

Farrell, E. E. (1921). Survey of Nationality of Children in Ungraded Classes. Ungraded VII, 2, 25-28.

Farrell, E. E. (1921). The Unclassified Child. Ungraded VIII, 5, 97-104.

Farrell, E. E. (1924). Mental Hygiene Problems of Maladjusted Children. Ungraded IX, 5, 99-108.

Farrell, E. E. (1924). Some Causes of Delinquency. Ungraded X, 2.

Farrell, E. E. (1925). What New York City Does for Its Problem Children. Ungraded XI, 5, 10-18.

Fernald, W. E. (1909, 1910). Imbecile With Criminal Instincts. Journal of Psycho-Asthenics, 14, 16-38.

Gelb, S. A. (1989). Not Simply Bad and Incorrigible: Science, Morality, and Intellectual Deficiency. History of Education Quarterly, 29(3), 359-379.

Goddard, H. H. (1917). Mental Tests and the Immigrants. Journal of Delinquency, 2, 243-277.

Hefferman, H. (1935). Meeting the Needs of Exceptional Children in Rural Schools. Exceptional Children, 2, 49.

Hendrick, I. G., & MacMillan, D. L. (1987). Coping With Diversity in City School Systems: The Role of Mental Testing in Shaping Special Classes for Mentally Retarded Children in Los Angeles, 1900-1930. Education and Training in Mental Retardation, 22, 10-17.

Hime, G. J. (1997). Seventy-Five Years of CEC Exceptional Service. TEACHING Exceptional Children, 29(5), 4.

Hoffman, E. (1975). The American Public Schools and the Deviant Child: The Origins of Their Involvement. Journal of Special Education, 9,(7), 415-523.

International Council for the Education of Exceptional Children. Ungraded XI, (5), 121.

Lord, F. E. (1981). The CEC Story. Chapter 2. Founding of the Council. (1922-1924). Exceptional Children, 47, 47-55.

Lord, F. E. (1976). Great Moments in the History of the Council for Exceptional Children. Exceptional Child Education at the Bicentennial: A Parade of Progress, 43, 32-36.

Minutes of Meeting of the Committee on Mental Hygiene. (1920). Ungraded V, 4, 84-85.

New York University. (1914, June 16). New York University Bulletin: School of Pedagogy, XIV, 16, 22, 48, 50-51.

New York University. (1921). Notes and News. Psychology Bulletin, 18, 439.

The Present Outlook Today. (1942). Journal of Exceptional Children, 8, 263-264.

Quotations: Elizabeth Farrell. (1932). School and Society, 36(939), 570-571.

Richardson, J. G. (1994, Winter). Common, Delinquent and Special: On the Formalization of Common Schooling in the American States. American Educational Research Journal, 31, 695-723.

Richardson, J. G., & Parker, T. L. (1993). The Institutional Genesis of Special Education: The American Case. American Journal of Education, 101, 359-392.

Safford, P. L., & Safford E. J. (1998, July/August). Visions of the Special Class. Remedial and Special Education, 19(4), 229-238.

Sargent, B. B. (1935). The International Council for Exceptional Children, Journal of Exceptional Children, 2, 32-38.

Sigmon, S. B. (1983, Summer). The History and Future of Educational Segregation. Journal for Special Educators, 19(4), 1-15.

Spalding, W. B., & Kvaraceus, W. C. (1914), Sex Discrimination in Special Class Placement. Exceptional Children, 11, 42-44.

Thomas, W. B. (1986). Mental Testing and Tracking for the Social Adjustment of an Urban Underclass, 1920-1930. Journal of Education, 168(2), 9-30.

Tropea, J. L. (1987, Spring). Bureaucratic Order and Special Children: Urban Schools, 1890s-1940s. History of Education Quarterly, 27(1), 29-53.

Ungraded I, 1. (1915, May).

Ungraded X, 1. (1925, May).

United Neighborhood Houses of New York, Henry Street Settlement. (n.d.). Retrieved February 23, 1999, from http://www.unhny.org/unh/mem_henry.htnl

Wald, L. D. (1936). Education and the Arts. Exceptional Children, 1, 82-87.

Warner, M. L. (1942). Early History of the International Council for Exceptional Children. Journal of Exceptional Children, 8, 244-247.

Warner, M. L. (1944). Founders of the International Council for Exceptional Children. Journal of Exceptional Children, 10, 217-223.

Wooden, H. Z. (1981). The CEC Story. Chapter 1. Growth of a Social Concept: An Overview. Exceptional Children, 47, 40-47.

Wooden, H. Z. (1935). The Spirit of the Pioneer. Exceptional Children, 1, 88.

Reports

Baltimore Board of School Commissioners. (1902). Annual Report. Baltimore, MD: Author.

Baltimore Board of School Commissioners. (1903). Annual Report. Baltimore, MD: Author.

Brown, E. G. (1905). Seventh Annual Report of the City Superintendent of Schools to the Board of Education, Appendix K: A Report on Special Classes for Defective Children. New York: New York City Board of Education.

City of Marcellus, NY. (1860). Town of Marcellus Census. Marcellus, NY: Author.

City of Oswego, NY. (1897-1898). Oswego City Directory. Oswego, NY: Author.

City of Oswego, NY. (1904). Oswego City Directory. Oswego, NY: Author.

City of Oswego, NY. (1906-1910). Oswego City Directory. Oswego, NY: Author.

City of Oswego, NY. (1912). Oswego City Directory. Oswego, NY: Author.

City of Oswego, NY. (1914). Oswego City Directory. Oswego, NY: Author.

City of Oswego, NY. (1916). Oswego City Directory. Oswego, NY: Author.

City of Oswego, NY. (1918-1923). Oswego City Directory. Oswego, NY: Author.

City of Oswego, NY. (1925-1927). Oswego City Directory. Oswego, NY: Author.

City of Oswego, NY. (1929). Oswego City Directory. Oswego, NY: Author.

City of Oswego, NY. (1931). Oswego City Directory. Oswego, NY: Author.

City of Oswego, NY. (1933). Oswego City Directory. Oswego, NY: Author.

City of Oswego, NY. (1935). Oswego City Directory. Oswego, NY: Author.

City of Oswego, NY. (1937). Oswego City Directory. Oswego, NY: Author.

City of Oswego, NY. (1939). Oswego City Directory. Oswego, NY: Author.

City of Utica, New York. (1870). Onieda County 9th Ward Census. Utica, NY: Author.

City of Utica, New York. (1870). Utica City Directory. Utica, NY: Author.

City of Utica, New York. (1872). Utica City Directory. Utica, NY: Author.

City of Utica, New York. (1880). Onieda County Census. Utica, NY: Author.

City of Utica, New York. (1885). Utica City Directory. Utica, NY: Author.

City of Utica, New York. (1893-1897). Utica City Directory. Utica, NY: Author.

City of Utica, New York. (1900). Onieda County 4th Ward Census. Utica, NY: Author.

City of Utica, New York. (1900). Utica City Directory. Utica, NY: Author.

Detroit Board of Education. (1897). Detroit Public Schools Annual Report. Detroit, MI: Author.

Ettinger, W. L. (1918-1920). Annual Report of the Superintendent of Schools to the Board of Education, Reports on Special Classes. New York: New York City Board of Education.

Farrell, E. E. (1903). Fifth Annual Report of the City Superintendent of Schools to the Board of Education, Appendix F: Report on Treatment of Defective Children in Great Britain. New York: New York City Board of Education.

Farrell, E. E. (1907). Ninth Annual Report of the City Superintendent of Schools to the Board of Education, Appendix V: Report on Education of Mentally Defective Children. New York: New York City Board of Education.

Farrell, E. E. (1908). Tenth Annual Report of the City Superintendent of Schools to the Board of Education, Appendix T: Report on Education of Mentally Defective Children. New York: New York City Board of Education.

Farrell, E. E. (1909). Eleventh Annual Report of the City Superintendent of Schools to the Board of Education, Appendix S: Education of Mentally Defective Children. New York: New York City Board of Education.

Farrell, E. E. (1910-1911). Thirteenth Annual Report of the City Superintendent of Schools to the Board of Education, Ungraded Classes: Report on Work for Mentally Defective Children. New York: New York City Board of Education.

Farrell, E. E. (1911-1912). Fourteenth Annual Report of the City Superintendent of Schools to the Board of Education, Reports on Defective Children: Ungraded Classes. New York: New York City Board of Education.

Farrell, E. E. (1912-1913). Fifteenth Annual Report of the City Superintendent of Schools to the Board of Education, Reports on Defective Children: Ungraded Classes. New York: New York City Board of Education.

Farrell, E. E. (1913-1914). Fifteenth Annual Report of the City Superintendent of Schools to the Board of Education, An Analysis of Dr. Goddard's School Inquiry Report on Ungraded Classes. New York: New York City Board of Education.

Farrell, E. E. (1913-1914). Sixteenth Annual Report of the City Superintendent of Schools to the Board of Education, Reports on Defective Children: Mental Defectives. New York: New York City Board of Education.

Farrell, E. E. (1914-1915). Seventeenth Annual Report of the City Superintendent of Schools to the Board of Education, Report on Defective Children: Ungraded Classes. New York: New York City Board of Education.

Farrell, E. E. (1915-1916). Eighteenth Annual Report of the City Superintendent of Schools to the Board of Education, Reports on Special Classes: Ungraded Classes. New York: New York City Board of Education.

Farrell, E. E. (1916-1917). Nineteenth Annual Report of the City Superintendent of Schools to the

Board of Education, Reports on Special Classes: Ungraded Classes. New York: New York City Board of Education.

Farrell, E. E. (1918-1920). Annual Report of the City Superintendent of Schools to the Board of Education, Reports on Special Classes: Ungraded Classes. New York: New York City Board of Education.

Farrell, E. E. (1921). Twenty-Third Annual Report of the Superintendent of Schools to the Board of Education, Reports on Special Classes: Ungraded Classes. New York: New York City Board of Education.

Farrell, E. E. (1925-1926). Twenty-Eighth Annual Report of the Superintendent of Schools to the Board of Education, Report of the Department of Ungraded Classes. New York: New York City Board of Education.

Farrell, E. E. (1929). Thirty-First Annual Report of the Superintendent of Schools to the Board of Education: Ungraded Classes. New York: New York City Board of Education.

Farrell, E. E. (1930). Thirty-Second Annual Report of the Superintendent of Schools to the Board of Education: Ungraded Classes. New York: New York City Board of Education.

Farrell, E. E. (1931). Thirty-Third Annual Report of the Superintendent of Schools to the Board of Education: Ungraded Classes. New York: New York City Board of Education.

Goddard, H. H. (1912). Report on the Educational Aspects of the Public School System of the City of New York to the Committee of School Inquiry of the Board of Estimates and Apportionment: Ungraded Classes. New York: New York City Board of Education.

Gullick. L. H., & Ayres, L. P. (1908). Tenth Annual Report of the City Superintendent of Schools to the Board of Education, Appendix S: Causes of Retardation of Pupils, An Investigation of Retardation of Fifteen Schools in New York City, Borough of Manhattan. New York: New York City Board of Education.

Maxwell, W. H. (1899). First Annual Report of the City Superintendent of Schools to the Board of Education. New York: New York City Board of Education.

Maxwell, W. H. (1900). Second Annual Report of the City Superintendent of Schools to the Board of Education. New York: New York City Board of Education.

Maxwell, W. H. (1901). Third Annual Report of the City Superintendent of Schools to the Board of Education. New York: New York City Board of Education.

Maxwell, W. H. (1902). Fourth Annual Report of the City Superintendent of Schools to the Board of Education. New York: New York City Board of Education.

Maxwell, W. H. (1903). Fifth Annual Report of the City Superintendent of Schools to the Board of Education. New York: New York City Board of Education.

Maxwell, W. H. (1904). Sixth Annual Report of the City Superintendent of Schools to the Board of Education. New York: New York City Board of Education.

Maxwell, W. H. (1905). Seventh Annual Report of the City Superintendent of Schools to the Board of Education. New York: New York City Board of Education.

Maxwell, W. H. (1906). Eighth Annual Report of the City Superintendent of Schools to the Board of Education. New York: New York City Board of Education.

Maxwell, W. H. (1907). Ninth Annual Report of the City Superintendent of Schools to the Board of Education. New York: New York City Board of Education.

Maxwell, W. H. (1908). Tenth Annual Report of the City Superintendent of Schools to the Board of Education. New York: New York City Board of Education.

Maxwell, W. H. (1909). Eleventh Annual Report of the City Superintendent of Schools to the Board of Education. New York: New York City Board of Education.

Maxwell, W. H. (1910). Twelfth Annual Report of the City Superintendent of Schools to the Board of Education. New York: New York City Board of Education.

Maxwell, W. H. (1911). Thirteenth Annual Report of the City Superintendent of Schools to the Board of Education. New York: New York City Board of Education.

Maxwell, W. H. (1912). Fourteenth Annual Report of the City Superintendent of Schools to the Board of Education. New York: New York City Board of Education.

Maxwell, W. H. (1913). Fifteeth Annual Report of the City Superintendent of Schools to the Board of Education. New York: New York City Board of Education.

Maxwell, W. H. (1914). Sixteenth Annual Report of the City Superintendent of Schools to the Board of Education. New York: New York City Board of Education.

Maxwell, W. H. (1915). Seventeenth Annual Report of the City Superintendent of Schools to the Board of Education. New York: New York City Board of Education.

Meleney, C. E. (1904). Sixth Annual Report of the City Superintendent of Schools to the Board of Education, Appendix C: Report on Compulsory Education. New York: New York City Board of Education.

New York University. (1914). New York University Directory. New York: Author

New York University. (1915). Directory of the Faculties of NYU. New York: Author.

New York University. (1916). Directory of the Council and Faculties. New York: Author.

Oneida City, NY. (1887-1888). Oneida City Directory. Oneida, NY: Author.

Oneida City, NY. (1891-1895). Oneida City Directory. Oneida, NY: Author.

O'Shea, W. J. (1925). Twenty-Seventh Annual Report of City Superintendent of Schools to the Board of Education. New York: New York City Board of Education.

O'Shea, W. J. (1926). Twenty-Eighth Annual Report of City Superintendent of Schools to the Board of Education. New York: New York City Board of Education.

O'Shea, W. J. (1927). Twenty-Ninth Annual Report of City Superintendent of Schools to the Board of Education. New York: New York City Board of Education.

O'Shea, W. J. (1928). Thirtieth Annual Report of City Superintendent of Schools to the Board of Education. New York: New York City Board of Education.

O'Shea, W. J. (1929). Thirty-First Annual Report of City Superintendent of Schools to the Board of Education. New York: New York City Board of Education.

O'Shea, W. J. (1931). Thirty-Third Annual Report of City Superintendent of Schools to the Board of Education. New York: New York City Board of Education.

Philadelphia Board of Education. (1897). Philadelphia School Report. Philadelphia, PA: Author.

Philadelphia Board of Education. (1909). Philadelphia School Report. Philadelphia, PA: Author.

Shallow, E. B. (1907). Ninth Annual Report of the City Superintendent of Schools to the Board of Education, Appendix F: Report on the Operation of the Compulsory Education Law. New York: New York City Board of Education.

Stevens, E. L. (1903). Fifth Annual Report of the City Superintendent of Schools to the Board of Education. New York: New York City Board of Education.

Straubenmuller, G. (1909). Eleventh Annual Report of the City Superintendent of Schools to the Board of Education, Appendix S: Vocation Schools and Classes for Mentally Defective Children. New York: New York City Board of Education.

Teachers College, Columbia University, NY. (1916-1934). School of Education Report, New York.

Superintendent of Schools of the City of Utica. (1881). Annual Report. Utica, NY: Author.

Superintendent of Schools of the City of Utica. (1895). Annual Report. Utica, NY: Author.

Superintendent of Schools of the City of Utica. (1896). Annual Report. Utica, NY: Author.

Superintendent of Schools of the City of Utica. (1897). Annual Report. Utica, NY: Author.

Superintendent of Schools of the City of Utica. (1898). Annual Report. Utica, NY: Author.

Walsh, E. A. (1932). Thirty-Fourth Annual Report of the Superintendent of Schools to the Board of Education: Ungraded Classes. New York: New York City Board of Education.

Walsh, E. A. (1933). Thirty-Fifth Annual Report of the Superintendent of Schools to the Board of Education: Ungraded Classes. New York: New York City Board of Education.

DATE DUE			

ELIZABETH FARRELL

FOUNDER OF THE
COUNCIL FOR EXCEPTIONAL CHILDREN

•

Did you know inclusion was a
concept that originated over a century ago?

•

Think issues such as assessment and finding
qualified special education teachers are new?

•

And who, exactly, was
Elizabeth Farrell?

Chances are, you won't see Elizabeth Farrell's name in most education textbooks. However, in the early 1900's her tireless devotion, her innovative ideas, and her long-range vision made her instrumental in the development of special education as we know it today.

In light of all she accomplished, it's important to remember that at the turn of the century women couldn't even vote. Tea parties and corsets were more the order of the day. Yet women were asserting themselves more than ever before, especially in the social reform arena. Elizabeth was one of those women. Elizabeth chose to work. She chose to turn her back on her family's fortune and work to change the educational structure of the public school system so that it addressed the needs of those children unable to succeed in the regular class setting.

And, she did.